My Path of Faith

A Life's Journey Learning to Love

Barbie Schuchart-Carlisle

My Path of Faith
Author, Barbie Schuchart-Carlisle
Copyright © 2018 by Barbie Schuchart-Carlisle. All Rights Reserved.

Published by:
Barbie Schuchart-Carlisle
All Rights Reserved. No part of this book may be used or reproduced in any manner whatsoever without the expressed written permission from the author. Send all inquiries to:

17426 Harris Rd., Defiance, OH 43512
Email: mypathoffaith@gmail.com

ISBN: 9780692056752

Printed In the United States of America
Scriptures marked NLT are taken from the New Living Translation (NLT): New Living Translation, public domain.

Dedication

I am dedicating my book to the one, the only, who has always been with me throughout my entire life; from as far back as I can remember to this very day. I am the one who has faltered and turned away, but Christ has always brought me back to Him. I've never stopped praying or talking to the one, I've always called "My Best Friend, My Father, My Lord and Savior, Jesus Christ."

I had to do one of the hardest things ever in my life. Here is what I wrote following the beginning of what I thought was the End for me. This is how "My Path of Faith" has always been in my life… I thought it was my end but He had made my plans long ago.

> "But my life is worth nothing to me unless I use it for finishing the work assigned me by the Lord Jesus—the work of telling others the Good News about the wonderful grace of God." (Acts of the Apostles 20:24, NLT)

I came here to hide but instead was found.

Thank you, Father, for never giving up on me.

Contents

Foreword 1
My Sweet Jesus 3
Prologue 5

Chapter 1: Life on the Farm, "God as My Friend" 11
Chapter 2: My "Imaginary Friend" Made a Home in My Heart 19
Chapter 3: Brokenness Opens a Path for Obedience 28
Chapter 4: Still Running from Me, Not towards the Light 37
Chapter 5: Enjoying Life a Little Too Much and Running on Fear 44
Chapter 6: God's Precious Surprise Gifts Can be a Blessing 47
Chapter 7: Strength to Protect my Children, Standing on My Own 51
Chapter 8: Experiencing the Love of Christ 53
Chapter 9: The Devil/Evil Is Working Overtime 62
Chapter 10: Seeing the Truth in Me Through Others 67
Chapter 11: Another Angel Is Gifted to Me 75
Chapter 12: Covered by the Blood of Jesus in the Darkest of Places 81

v

Chapter 13:	Mother Mary Comes to Me Speaking Words of Wisdom	94
Chapter 14:	Learning to Love through Jesus' Eyes	99
Chapter 15:	Letting Go of Anger; Having a Forgiving Heart	110
Chapter 16:	An Amazing Calling for a Journey to New Jersey	117
Chapter 17:	Serving God's Children from around the World	124
Chapter 18:	Starting Over in Kentucky, Again Heading toward My Ending	128
Chapter 19:	My First Glimpse of Domestic Violence	139
Chapter 20:	God Sends His Angels to Me	147
Chapter 21:	Completely Broken by Domestic Violence	152
Chapter 22:	He Thought I Was Worth Saving, so He Cleaned Me Up Inside	159
Chapter 23:	God Blesses Me Abundantly beyond My Dreams	174
Chapter 24:	Making My Peace with the Past	180
Chapter 25:	Jesus Continues to Visit and Now I Listen	183
Chapter 26:	Is This the End?	189
Chapter 27:	Who Am I Now?	191
Epilogue		193

Foreword

As you will learn, many things have happened in my life that were both good and bad. Though I've been through a lot, for me, this was one of the hardest things I've had to walk through. On March 28, 2016, while on a family vacation in Sanford, Florida the man I thought I loved almost beat me to death after dropping my son off at the airport. Afterwards, I unfortunately, tried to go home by drinking antifreeze. I'll explain this in more detail later in my journey.

I've almost died several times from indoor mold exposure and, those who said they loved me (including my family), said I was faking when I was very ill. All the while, it was either being scraped off the inside of my lungs, or I was on oxygen helping me to breathe. I was abused by my mother as a child verbally, emotionally, and mentally. To this day, she still hates me. She never hit me, but that would've been easier to get over then being told that you're no good, you're ugly, I don't want you, you're a slut, I don't like you and I'm going to give you away because I don't want you.

I was date raped at sixteen, attempted raped and burglarized at seventeen. I attempted suicide a few times and was homeless for eight months. These are just a very small portion of what I've been through in my life. I've felt and been so lost, hopeless and alone as if God forgot about me. I knew He was there and loved me, but why were these horrible things happening to me? Other people doing horrible things were living carefree, happy and wonderful lives.

One of my counselors recommended a church about a month after I moved to where I'm now living. Since I moved here from

Kentucky, I felt myself being pulled to the very same church every time I drove past. However, due to the bad experience I had with the pastor at the church I worked at in Kentucky for eight years, I hadn't been able to go back to any church. My PTSD had left me scared of doing many things. However, I went on Sunday, June 16, 2016!

The minute that I walked through the doors, I looked to the back of the sanctuary, I took a deep breath, exhaled and started crying. I felt the Holy Spirit surround me and fill me up again and then I said Oh, Thank you Father, I'm home. I've never felt "at home" anywhere in my life.

I cried thru the entire service. It was as if it was just for me. I felt every question I had over the past two and a half months (since the beating March 28, 2016), were being answered. Most of all, I am His and He loves me! I left there with HOPE for the first time in a year and a half! I felt full of the Holy Spirit again, no longer was I empty, or lost and alone!

To be continued towards the end of the book!

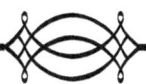

My Sweet Jesus

I came to you long before
I realized just who you were.

As a 'lil girl I always whispered
My fears and secrets
In Your imaginary ear.
Somehow knowing in my heart,
You were always there,
Catching each teardrop.

I never questioned
When the answer came.
It was just your breath upon my hair.
A gentle nudge
I'd hold so dear,
And knew so well.

Talking for hours
Running thru the fields
Or kneeling, crying out in pain.
Wrapped in your loving embrace
I'd always find in you
Peace and comfort
Like no other place.

Half a century now has passed,
You're the one true constant
Still holding true.

BARBIE SCHUCHART-CARLISLE

You let me waver,
Or so I thought,
You never turned away—
Instead, My Sweet Jesus,
You always carried me,
In your tender, loving arms.

As I've grown thru the years,
You've shown me,
Just who you are, and now;
You want me to teach others
By showing them, your Love.
What an awesome Honor
Thank You, My Sweet Jesus!

Barbie Schuchart-Carlisle
August 18, 2013

Prologue

As you read my book, please remember this:

> "For many years I believed everything bad happening to me was because my own mother couldn't love me. I thought I'd done something horribly wrong, which I couldn't remember and was to be punished all my life for it. Because of this shame and pride, I made bad decisions over and over allowing others to use it against me and rob me of my life.
>
> However, as I walked My Path of Faith, I've learned, "I'm a survivor, an overcomer," and it is only because of my blind, undying faith and "Christ in me," that I know I am all of this!"

This book will tell about my life, which will include many people who have come and gone through my life some good, and some bad. What I say others did in my life, is in no way a judgment on them or what they did. My goal in this is for you, the reader, to see how I always had God in my life. At a very early, young age, even without knowing it, I gave my life to God. My entire life has been dedicated to Him. What I wanted out of life was to be allowed to have some amazing, beautiful children and to raise them with their knowing I loved them more than life itself. I tried to do this, but I am only human, and there were obstacles, like me.

We all make mistakes. We try to do better. We make amends, if possible. I would give up my life and soul for any one of my three children. I miss seeing them, talking to them, and being a part of their lives. Life goes by too quickly. I've prayed every day to be reunited with them. I know that they are covered in the Blood of Jesus, and one day, we will be together again. In one of my prayers, I was given the answer as I was on my knees crying for them. I felt Him answer. He said, "My dear child, I loved them long before I entrusted them to you. I love them more than you could ever understand, just as I love you. I will keep them safe on their journeys in life until it is time for them to come back to you. Right now, do My work, and I will reward you in the end. Now, go forth as I have told you, knowing they are safe and loved." I cried so hard. It wasn't because I knew they were gone, but because I knew they were safe and loved and, I too was loved. I was at peace knowing He held them and I was able to let go and let them walk their paths in this life. It hurts I won't lie. Yes, I long for them, but I trust completely in my Lord.

What I'm going to tell you about my life, is about "my journey only, *My Path of Faith*." I will not tell you about every single moment of my life, only about "moments of my life, in phases of my life." At the end of each chapter, I will point out myself where I found Jesus/God in my life throughout that time. I pray that through your reading of my book you too may look back on your life and find Jesus/God working in your life.

One time, talking to my mother, she asked me, "Why can't you just settle down in one place?" I'm asked this question quite often. Why did you go there, or why did you come back? Why did you move? Why did you quit that job? I've thought about this and have written a lot on it. When I felt answers that Sunday, this was one of them, "I've been in places for periods of time, but nowhere that I ever would've called home. Never have I had friends, except one, who's been a best friend for a long time. I've never 'belonged anywhere or fit in.'" My answer was simple, "I've been doing God's work!" "I was obeying Him!" When He placed it upon my heart to go (new job, a new place to live, follow someone, or go to someone, etc.), I just went. It is just that simple. Often times, it would be revealed to me before. Sometimes, I'd have to wait until I was deep in the middle of the "mess" before it was revealed! You will understand all of this later in the book!

When I walked into church, Sunday, standing at the entrance of the sanctuary, seeing the cross, I said, "Thank you, Father, I'm home." That was the first time in my life I felt at home.

He began the next week giving me more messages through an amazing woman named Angie. There were more messages to come. The hate that I had for the man who beat me was removed. Amazing people started coming into my life, and good things started happening. I had tried to leave to go to Florida or back to Kentucky, but God had other plans. He'd had them all along and had only been waiting for me. He'd placed on my heart; "Daughter, you are home for now." I know my next stop is with Him, my eternal home. I was then graced with a job of being useful to someone else. This job came from my angel at church. I was told I'd been an answer to their prayers! They were an answer to my prayers! I have no desire to move anywhere now. I no longer have to run. If God needs me or calls on me, I still continue to do His bidding, to do whatever He lays upon my heart.

Where Is God in My Path of Faith?

Where do I see God in this! This is only the beginning! Do you see Him yet? If not, keep reading! If so, keep reading! He was there waiting for me. The Holy Spirit again filled me as I walked into the church to let me know, "God is with you Barbie and He has always been with you!" There's so much more of Him to come! I tried to die to be with my Father, but He had other plans!

Scripture

> God saved you by his grace when you believed. And you can't take credit for this; it is a gift from God. Salvation is not a reward for the good things

we have done, so none of us can boast about it. For we are God's masterpiece, He has created us anew in Christ Jesus, so we can do the good things He planned for us long ago. (Ephesians 2:8–10, NLT)

Praise

Thank you, Father, for your love, grace, and believing in me. Thank you for creating me anew through Christ Jesus. For planning out my life better than I could ever have dreamed. Jesus, thank you, for your amazing, selfless gift of my salvation.

MY PATH OF FAITH

This is just to give you an idea of the town I grew up in, here is a picture of "Old Loveland" in 1992! Loveland is not the same now as it was then. It has become quite a big, thriving city! The little store on the right, Millitzer's is where our family bought our shoes! The Whistle Stop was the local and only bar/restaurant!

"This area was called, Old Loveland" and this was in 1992! The little store on the right, Millitzer's is where our family bought our shoes! The Whistle Stop on the left, was the local and only bar/restaurant, we never went there!

The farmhouse where we grew up was on 176 acres. Ten acres of it was a garden where Mom and we kids canned, froze and grew what we ate. We had a milk cow that my little sister, Bonnie, and I milked. Our cows were sent to the butcher, the chickens, we did ourselves. We had three greenhouses, a huge fishing lake, pool, and Dad managed sixteen banks as his "real job!" Mom would sew all of our clothes (until I learned to sew my own!). Every day of the week was scheduled with a different chore. No need for employees, five kids were all that was needed! In all honesty, my family lived in our own little world, all alone from the outside world. I thought life was perfect,

This is where I lived for 17 years growing up.

except there was something wrong with me, and I couldn't figure out what it was. Why would my own mother hate me? But Dad adored me. We did have fun, and there was laughter. But, always lying underneath in my heart and soul was such a sad loneliness of needing my mother's love that would never come.

Chapter 1

Life on the Farm, "God as My Friend"

It would be great if I could tell you, I'm one of those who remembers every detail about when I was a little child and everything was wonderful. However, there are quite a few memories that are forever burned into my memory. They are like a movie playing in my mind. I can actually see and feel them happening as I tell them. As you can imagine, some are wonderful, loving, and happy. Others, well, I don't like to tell them or talk about them too much. I've been told of incidents that I completely do not recall. I am assuming that I have just erased them, blocked them out, as so many of us do when we've had so much hurt and pain.

What I do remember as a child is that I was always alone. I did not fit in with my brothers and sisters or, more importantly, my mother or grandmother; my mom's mom who we called "Mema." They all had each other; my two brothers, Steve, the oldest from Mom's first marriage, and my other brother, Jimmy, from Mom and Dad's marriage. Then there was Debi, the oldest girl from Mom's first marriage, and Bonnie, the youngest and from Mom and Dad's marriage. Then there was me, the middle child, from Mom and Dad's marriage and middle daughter from their joining marriage. The black sheep of our family! Dad had another daughter, who he never saw after his divorce because of his ex-wife and her mother. Jimmy, Bonnie, and I never knew of the other marriages until my seventh grade of school.

Mom sat me down to give the big "sex talk" telling me that she and Dad had been married before. Her husband had a head-on collision with a telephone pole on Christmas Eve after they had a drunken fight when he took off driving. He died instantly. Steve and Debi were around seven and three. So during Mom's "sex talk" with me, she advised me that Steve and Debi were my "half-brother and sister." I had another half-sister, Carin, from Dad's first marriage! Now, at this age, having been so isolated all my life, I had no idea of sex or alcoholism. I thought that this was what the big talk was supposed to be! I was just happy Mom was finally talking to me!

From what was told, Dad grew up in Northern Kentucky with fifteen siblings. Dad's father came straight over from Germany, married my grandma, who was an Indian woman here in America. However, she died at an early age after having fifteen kids. Grandpa married again to a German woman in Kentucky who we called "Floating Florence!" I do not even know if this was her real name! I do not know much about my Grandpa except for the fact that his family owned a candy factory in Germany called, "Schuchart Chocolate Factory!" Mom's family landed in New York from Scotland. While driving through the streets of New York in their car, they were watching people leaping from buildings to their deaths. This was the day of the Great Stock Market Crash! "Welcome to America!" My grandmother known as "Mema," had two sisters, Aunt Marg and Aunt Agnes. Mom was an only child. I do not believe that I ever met Mema's mother, but I do remember hearing them talk about her.

Mom's family lived in Mariemont, Ohio. Dad's family lived in Erlanger, Kentucky. Dad was a big basketball player all through school. His name was always in the paper as "Sugar Schuchart" and/or "Lefty Schuchart!" He was a very ambitious man! He received a scholarship for basketball and went to Eastern Kentucky University for his master's degree in finance/accounting and business and, of course, to play basketball! Unfortunately, after a year, he blew out his knee and was no longer able to play. He did continue his education and graduated. He then served in the Army in World War II. Dad began working at a very young age doing any job he could hustle! He talked about driving a truck around for the Deusing brothers at the age of twelve delivering ice blocks for customer's iceboxes. After college, he went into real estate, banking, hotels, casinos, and investments, anything he could get into. He invented a unique aluminum siding house in Erlanger, Kentucky. There are only two of them in the world and they are on the National Historical Register! Dad then went on to the banking business and excelled very quickly. In a short period, he became the manager of sixteen savings and loans banks across Ohio and Kentucky. The Bank was called Capital Financial Savings!

One of his offices was located in Loveland, Ohio, where Mom came in for a loan. Very little has been told of their dating and relationship, but Dad said that he gave Mom a loan as she was a widow with two little children. Dad then asked her out and soon afterward, they were married. Dad was taking care of Mom and her two children, raising them as if they were his own. He found the farmhouse in Loveland, a mere 176 acres for $25,000. Back then, this was "very expensive," but Dad purchased it with cash for his new family. His banking friends told him he was crazy for paying that much money for something way out in the middle of nowhere! Dad always wanted out of Kentucky! He also had an office in downtown Cincinnati, Ohio. When the cobblestone streets in downtown Cincinnati were torn up to make the new blacktop ones, Dad brought home truckloads and built a fireplace in our formal living room! He had built on many additions to the house and was always improving the farm.

Many years later when Dad divorced Mom after forty years of marriage, he sold the house. The person who bought it had to pay to live on ten acres of the land. He sold the House alone for a mere $699,000.00! He'd already earlier given Jimmy, Debi, and her husband acreage to build and live on with their families. Dad had since built two additional houses, and they moved next door from one to the other, selling the last one as they moved. Everything was sold by the time of the divorce. Dad had also sold off other acreage over the years. I might be wrong, but I think he had a pretty good return on his investment! Dad was just that way! He could turn a penny into gold!

I'm sure you can tell by now that I absolutely adored my Dad, and he adored me as his little girl! Everyone knew that I was Daddy's little girl! Dad was actually harder and tougher on me than he was on the other four kids. He did it to help mold me into the person I am today. He was preparing me for life and helping me get through my childhood with Mom and Mema. He told me, later in life, that he always knew I would have a harder life and would have to be tougher than my brothers and sisters. He said that was why he gave my brothers and sisters' loans and property to help them get started. and he didn't help me. He knew I had to do it on my own with God. God wanted me to go through it by myself to walk my path with Him, not with handouts from "Daddy."

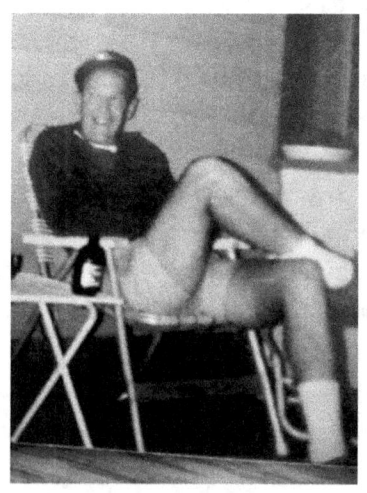

My Dad, Bill Schuchart, whom I loved very much.

I can never remember Mom telling me that I did anything good or that I was okay, just as I am. I've never really understood how it came about or when it started, but I can never remember *not* having my God in my life. I always talked to Him as if He were my best friend, in my thoughts and out loud, as a child does. I did not know that I was even praying back then. At a very young age, I started writing poetry to let out my feelings. To this day, I can wake up and the writing is just there, I have to get it out on paper. It's like a fire burning; you just have to get it out of you! To me, this is a Gift that I've been given from God.

I never shared these with anyone because Mom always made fun of me or told me that it was stupid and that I was crazy for talking with an imaginary, God-like friend. But then, she'd make comments to me telling me that she'd been up all night praying to have something bad happen to me. She would tell me I needed to be better, more like Bonnie and Debi. I needed to be prettier because I was ugly. Then she'd yell at me and sometimes smack me in a store then send me to the car saying I was making the boys look at me! I was so confused, having absolutely no idea what she was even talking about: why boys were looking at me. How did I make them look at me? What is wrong with me that they are looking at me and not my sisters? All my siblings, Dad, and Mom all had brown eyes and either black or dark brown hair. I was the only one with blonde hair and blue eyes.

Dad said I'd been born with red hair, and it had turned blonde. It was a joke in our family how much Dad loved redheaded women. I truly thought that I was adopted because I was so different from all of them. I had one cousin on Dad's side that had blonde hair. My two sisters were always a little heavier, and I was always extremely tiny and underweight. Mom would sew all of our clothes, and they all pretty much looked the same. What I saw in the mirror when I looked was what Mom told me I was. So, at the early age of four, I learned how to sew so that I could start sewing my own. Even at that early age, I started overachieving in everything to try to make Mom love me and not hate me.

Whenever Dad was home, I was always at his side. I worked in the fields, the greenhouses, shoveled manure; it didn't matter as long as I was with him. He taught me so much. He was so patient and loving with me. I loved building fences, buildings, tearing down anything, working in the hot sun, rain, and playing in the mud or the freezing cold just as long as I was with him! He always called me Tweety for his sweetie! I used to hate it when I had to go indoors and help Mom and my sisters clean or work around the house or doing anything with them. Mom would always go behind me redoing everything I did telling me how I did it wrong. When I worked with Dad, if I did something wrong, he would explain what I did wrong. Then we would do it right together, or he'd tell me how to do it right so I could fix it. I always felt good about myself with what I was doing and didn't feel as if I was a failure at everything. He taught me how to fish, bait my own hook, ride a motorcycle, and play sports like a boy! I loved being outside and still do to this day! Yes, I had my God, and I had Daddy, who was all I thought I ever needed, and they would never abandon me.

I always felt like I was in competition with my sister Bonnie. Mom was always comparing us to each other even if we weren't aware of this until we were adults. I went to her and made amends to her for spraying Lysol in her face. She and I were fighting one day when we were "cleaning the house." I, of course, had just been told that I was polishing wrong. I needed to do it more like Bonnie. Bonnie did a perfect job! Mom walked away. I only saw red. I hated Bonnie so much at that minute because she was "so perfect" in Mom's eyes. I was holding the can of Lysol. She looked at me, smiled with her big, beautiful, brown eyes, and told me, "You should be more like me, you do everything wrong!" I just took the can of Lysol and sprayed it in her face and eyes. She screamed, cried, and ran to Mom. I hated her because Mom loved her more than me. She was right; I could do nothing to change this. I honestly hated myself more than I could ever have hated her. All this did was make me hate myself even more. I ran outside and climbed up my tree crying; asking God to please let her be okay. I didn't really want to hurt her. I wanted to disappear and go away instead of hurting her. Mom loved her not me. I stayed hiding up in my tree the rest of the day until Dad came home that night.

When I was ten, I walked out onto the front porch where Mom was planting red and white striped Impatiens between the bushes. I do not know to this day, why I went out there, but when I went outside, she said to me, "I just want you to know I've talked to your father, and we've decided to give you away. I just can't stand having you anymore." Needless to say, I was stunned. I did my usual that I always did after her verbal abuse. I went to my room where I had a nut picker, I dug at my wrists, and arms to make the pain of her words go away. While doing this, I'd be crying out to God to take the pain away. Why can't I please her? What is wrong with me? What does she want me to do? When I cut myself, it's almost like "I become conscious again," my wrists would bleed, and I'd have deep gashes in them, but I'd never feel the pain from them; only the pain from the words spoken from this woman who is supposed to love me as her daughter. I could not even comprehend what was so wrong with me that my own mother couldn't even love me.

Over the years, I had asked her several times, why she had told me this. Why had she wanted to get rid of me? She said I was lying; she had never said that. I learned that this would be a normal thing for her. However, I thought I was losing my mind. When I talked to Bonnie many years later to make amends with her, she volunteered the information. Bonnie said, "Barbie, do you remember that day when you went out on the front porch and Mom said to you, 'Barbie, I just want you to know that I spoke with your father, and we are going to get rid of you?'"

I said, "Yes."

Bonnie said, "I was right beside the door, and I thought, OMG, if they're going to get rid of 'Little Miss Goody-Two-Shoes,' what will they do to me?"

I was so relieved to hear this; you just can't imagine. I was then able to let it go!

Where Is God in My Path of Faith?

God gave Dad the insight, whether he knew or not, to see that I had a long, hard road ahead of me. However, God was also in it for the long haul with me. Dad saw Mom treating me bad but didn't know the true extent. I also could have blinded my sister, but God showed us His grace. In my heart, God showed me; I truly didn't hate her. I hated myself but didn't understand why. Why I was so unlovable to a woman that was supposed to be my mother. I knew, without knowing, God loved me, even if I didn't understand. I could have easily died each time I dug at my wrists with the nut picker, even if that was not my intent. God already had a plan for my life! He had Barbie Schuchart's Life Journey, already planned out! I was learning each day to believe in and go to only "Him" and no one else.

Scripture:

> Dear children, let's not merely say that we love each other; let us show the truth by our actions.
> (1 John 3:18, NLT)

Praise

Thank you, Father, for so many blessings before I even knew that they were. You began to work with and through me at such a young age. Thank you for giving Dad wisdom even if he wasn't aware. Thank you for being my "imaginary friend" before I knew you were my "All."

Chapter 2

My "Imaginary Friend" Made a Home in My Heart

My childhood wasn't all doom and gloom. I played sports, took ballet and gymnastics. I was good at all that I did. Our two front yards were each the size of a football field. I would go out there and do flips up and down them. Dad even made balance beams out of railroad ties for me! We had horses, and I would go out and ride my horse in the fields, climbs trees, fish in our pond, or

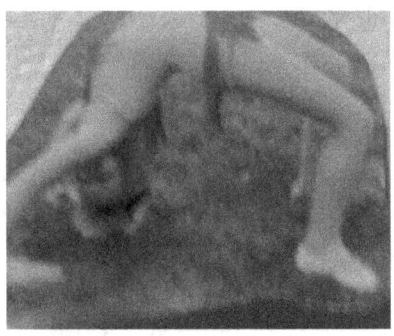

This is a picture of me doing some of my gymnastics!

swim in our pool. Our family wanted for nothing. We lived off the farm, raised cattle, chickens, and many other animals. I had many cats. One time, I actually had thirty-three of them! We worked very hard from sun up to sun down on the farm and in the greenhouses. I milked a cow; we made forts in the hayloft. But, everything had to be only with our family. No friends or outsiders were ever allowed. Our meals were three times a day. Every day of the week was routine, with the same things steak, potatoes, and a vegetable. Everything we ate was either grown in the garden, raised in the fields, and we made it all ourselves! If it was from the garden, it was fresh, frozen or canned.

Monday through Thursday, we had steak, salad or vegetable, and potato. Friday, it was hamburgers, BLT, some type of sandwich and soup or odd thing. Saturday, it was chili or spaghetti (which was actually spaghetti squash from the garden); and, Sunday was always chicken (in the summer Dad always grilled). When I left home, I didn't eat steak for years! We even made our ketchup! Anyone who knows me knows how much I love ketchup. I always took too much! Mom would make me sit there and eat all of it with a spoon, thinking it was a punishment! It wasn't! Our ketchup was sweet, not tangy and very good!

In the summer occasionally, we would have a hootenanny. For those who do not know what this is a Hootenanny was also an old Southern country word for "party." Nowadays, the word most commonly refers to a folk music party with an open microphone, at which different performers are welcome to get up sing and play an instrument in front of an audience. We didn't have a microphone! Instead, my brother, Steve, would play the guitar while we would all sing and dance outside on the back porch. This is one of the sweetest memories I have and cherish.

I've always been a little bit of a prankster. One night in the winter, Dad came home from work, and I was waiting for him in his bedroom with my fingers wrapped around his light switch. He went to flip the switch, making contact with my hand, not knowing I was there, it almost gave him a heart attack! One time, Mom was mad at me and came yelling for me. I ran, climbed up the big tree in the backyard, and hid above her laughing. She had no idea I was up there. I'd laugh and pray to Jesus, "Please keep me safe from her." One night, Mom was mad at me, for what, I have no idea. They were all going into town for the carnival. She told me I couldn't go. They left, and I went out and sat by the lake talking to God and listening to the frogs. I talked to God and the animals a lot, especially the chickens and a favorite rooster. I had a great idea! I caught about six frogs, took them inside, and put them under Mom's pillow and her sheets on her side of the bed.

Two weeks went by, and I didn't hear anything. Finally, I asked Bonnie if she heard anything about some frogs. Bonnie asked me, did you do that? My response, do what? The frogs apparently went from the bed through the registers into the laundry room into the washer. Dad was so puzzled on how frogs got into the washer. Bonnie ran out and told him what I did. Dad laughed so hard! Now, as an adult, not that I love frogs that much, but I have pictures that I've created and even made t-shirts with the frog logo on it. I even have a poem that goes with this that I have framed! To me, I started saying, F.R.O.G. meant, "Fully relying on God!"

F.R.O.G. I put frogs in mom's bed sheets because I was mad at her! From then on I started using this as Fully Relying On God!

One of my greatest memories of Dad is sitting on his lap, eating peanuts, pickled pig's feet, and watching Lawrence Welk. We went to church every Sunday, taking joy rides afterward. Dad would drive us going up and down hills making us laugh! He called this our "tummy ticklers!" At church, all I remember is playing with Mom's rosary holder. It was a Catholic Mass, and they spoke in Latin. I don't think I ever really put "My God" and the church together.

This is me as a little girl standing by our lake.

My God was my friend, my Savior. I talked to Him all the time and listened when He talked to me. He always helped me through the hard, difficult times.

We had a big lake that Dad handmade. We fished, swam, and in the wintertime, we would ice skate and I loved to figure skate and dance on it. We had horses that we would ride, and we'd play sports with each other, as well as, with Dad. Eventually, Dad built a large in-ground swimming pool for us. Bonnie and I loved to swim and lay out by the pool after we finished our chores. We would look at the clouds making believe we were floating up there while making them into different shapes. A couple of times, we were even allowed to camp out in a tent in the front yard. I remember many times when we had finished our chores; I would either take off and hide in the woods exploring or jump on my horse to go riding for hours in the woods. When we were old enough, Jimmy had built go-carts for us to race and ride. I'd go ramping and racing the dirt bikes with my brothers. I was always in the barn, helping dad with the animals, and as you can see, even had a favorite rooster!

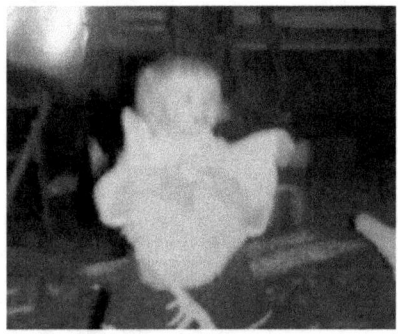
Me holding my favorite rooster that I use to play with.

Though I love playing sports I was always doing gymnastics, or ballet anytime, anywhere that I could! I'd spend many hours alone as a child; in my mind, I was sharing them with my best friend, God. I talked to Him at all times because my brothers and sisters had each other or they had Mom. If I ever had anyone, it would be either God or Bonnie. So, I talked to God, or I wrote to Him in my poetry.

The funny thing about making a "person/human" a "god figure," they are always going to be human and fail you. Dad was no exception to this. I do know without a doubt to this day that Dad loved me. He tried his best to protect me from Mom, my brothers, sisters, and then to prepare me for the cruelty the world was about to take upon my soul. He was harder on me than he was on any of my siblings. I can even remember one day looking at my Daddy and God revealing to me that "he is only my human Daddy," and he too will fail me. God also showed me that He is my only "True Father that will never leave nor forsake me." I won't lie, this hurt and scared me!

With the greenhouses and our farm, there was not a day that we didn't work. Dad also had his banking job, which makes him work even harder. I've also failed to mention that Dad had several houses that he owned, maintained, and rented in Loveland. He would take a vacation each summer for one month to catch up on the farm and various other works needing to be caught up. One day we would take off and go to LeSourdsville Lake. Back then, this was the "Kings Island Amusement Park!" Life was so simple and easy, so we were told! Though for us, it was still very hard. All of our life, it seemed all we did was school and work. Whether we worked in the greenhouse (every day), our daily chores around the farm, or in the house, it was always work, work, work! Our lives were planned out very carefully by Mom. She'd have these episodes where we were told that she was, "sick." She'd be in bed for anywhere from a day to a week, and Dad would take care of us. Other than that, everything was very routine, even our eating. It was like robots and clockwork!

LeSourdsville Lake Amusement Park is where we went for a day every summer as our summer vacation. We thought it was the best vacation on earth!

We always had to show affection to our parents in the way of kissing them goodbye or goodnight as they did with each other. Other than that, there was no affection in our home. Dad would hug and hold Bonnie and me or we'd sit on his lap in the evenings, but that's pretty much it. Bonnie and I saw Mom and Dad hold hands one time and were amazed at it. I remember talking to God, asking Him to help me learn to love more and in a different way when I had a family. I also asked Him to help me to learn to love others more through Jesus' eyes. And to learn how to show them love, but not like my mom shows love to us.

Mom told me, on a daily basis, that I was ugly and no good and would be nothing. I talked to God about this all the time, asking Him since I'm so ugly and bad, would He please help me to be a better person on the inside. Let me be better toward others and love others better than Mom does me. I wouldn't care about how ugly I was, I'd take care of my outside, but I'd let Him worry about my ugliness because I just wanted to be beautiful on the inside for Him. I hated looking in mirrors at myself and did for most of my life. All I saw was the ugly child that Mom saw. When I went to try out for cheerleading in seventh grade, that morning upon leaving, she said to me, "I was up all night praying that you don't make it. You know I get what I pray for." I didn't make it. I was told it was because my voice wasn't loud enough. I have a very soft, quiet voice to this day!

This is me in 7th grade. It is when I prayed to God and told him I wouldn't care about how ugly I was, I'd take care of my outside, and I'd let Him worry about my ugliness because I just wanted to be beautiful on the inside for Him.

I had no friends. I knew everyone, and everyone knew me. I wasn't allowed to have friends over or go to their homes. So, I was never invited. I was the "weird farm girl." I remember in seventh grade some girls and boys asked me to go to Kings Island with them for the Halloween Fest. I'd never been asked to do or go anywhere with anyone. I didn't really think I'd be allowed to, but I asked Dad and then Mom. Unbelievably, Dad said yes, so Mom had to. The morning before I left, Mom said to me, "I had dreams last night that something very bad is going to happen to you. I do not want you to go." Great, here we go again, just like the cheerleading thing, right. I told her I was going.

I had a great time for once in my childhood with other kids. It started storming, so we hung out in the shops for a while. I was walking around just looking because, of course, Mom gave no extra money. A few officers came up to me and said that I needed to go with them. I was startled, and it terrified me but, asking them what was wrong they only said, "Follow us please." They led me to a set of trailers and had me go inside with them. They searched me and found a brush in my sock. They asked me where I got it. I said, "It's my little sister, Bonnie's. She let me borrow it today and you can call home and ask her." They told me it wouldn't be necessary. I was almost in tears at this point. (You'll learn soon about my dime store incident at four years old) They explained to me that my "friends" were stealing from the shops. I was the only one that was "free to go!" Great! Now what! When I got home, I received the, "See, I told you, you would do something horrible," from Mom! Wouldn't you think she would have been proud of me?

No one but God knew how I suffered on the inside. I appeared strong, but in truth, I was a very scared little girl. My strength was and is always only from God.

Remember, at home, it was Debi and Bonnie with Mom, Steve, and Jimmy then it was me. When Dad was there and if he was working or had the time, I could be with him. I had no ally at home or school. God *was* my ally. I turned inward more and more. I learned later in life that the people at school thought that I was "stuck-up!"

When in fact, I was just terrified and believed I was ugly and no good like Mom told me. I thought I wasn't good enough for anyone! Mom drank cheap wine through a straw on a daily basis. Bonnie and I hated having to go and talk to her because she'd be sitting at the table crying, "Poor is me," slobbering drunk. Then we'd be stuck sitting listening to her. It got so bad that one night Bonnie and I were hiding in the living room closet. Mom and Dad were fighting. Dad was yelling at her, smashing all of her wine bottles. He told her if she's going to drink, stop buying the cheap wine, and he'd buy her gin instead! (Yea, that helped a lot!) Bonnie and I were terrified that night.

We'd never seen anything like that from them. They never showed any emotions let alone fighting like this. Dad bought Mom some gin! The gin didn't help her. It just got worse. Mom was like a different person at different times. One day, she was yelling at me in the produce department of the grocery store, she was relentless. Someone walked up to her and said, "Hi, Anne."

She was all of a sudden sweet as honey, just gushing sweetness. I promised God that day I would never be like her. I would always be just as I am. Not hurt anyone, at least not intentionally, but always be me, as He wants me to be. I would never pretend to be something other than whom or what I am.

As time went on, Steve was drafted to Vietnam. Debi got married and built a house in a field next to our property. I started working at the bakery in town. Debi's husband started cornering Bonnie and me individually, and trying to have his way with us, putting his hands on us. No matter what we told him, it never stopped. He would tell me about all of his affairs he had on my sister. It made me sick for her. I've only told a few people about this. She'd never believe me anyway. Bonnie and I discussed it because we both couldn't stand what he was doing to her or us. He eventually left Debi for someone else. He told her he had slept with me! Now, my own sister won't talk to me because she believes him! Even my brother used to make

Bonnie and I walk around in his bedroom modeling for him in our panties. Then he'd make me stand and turn and let him touch me. After this happened a few times, I felt so dirty and bad and wouldn't do it anymore. My Uncle Bob would take me on piggyback rides and lock his fingers together holding them upwards. I told Dad that it didn't feel good, and I didn't want him to do this. We never saw my Uncle Bob again. I thought Dad would always be my protector! I pray a lot to God for the healing of this family.

Where Is God in My Path of Faith?

God was always there when I talked to Him. He was my imaginary friend before I knew who He was. I went to Him for everything. I asked Him to help me when I hurt. I asked Him at this young age to work on me, on my insides/personality and, to be a better person. Please help me to learn to love through Jesus' eyes. To learn to love others in a different way than how Mom loved me. Dad was showing me a different love. I was being shown tough love by him but I was also being raised with good morals, values and work ethics even if I didn't know it at the time.

Scripture

> Then Christ will make his home in your hearts as you trust in him. Your roots will grow down into God's love and keep you strong. (Ephesians 3:17, NLT)

Praise

Thank you, Father, for being my "All." Thank you for always showing me true love.

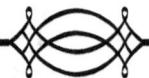

Chapter 3

Brokenness Opens a Path for Obedience

All through school, I knew everyone, and everyone knew me. I stayed to myself talking to God, reading, and writing and trying to be perfect for Mom. All through school and work to this day, I never miss even if I'm sick. In school, I only missed half a day. Truthfully, I wanted to go to school to get away from Mom. I acted as if I was happy and outgoing when I was just a terrified child who thought I wasn't worth anything. I started working at a bakery in Loveland. It was yet another escape for me from Mom. Just like talking to God, writing my poetry and reading was my escape.

I feel like I lived in a make-believe world with my God and writing. Mom always accused me of drinking and doing drugs and always tore apart my bedroom looking for this. What she didn't know or maybe she did and just refused to believe it, is that it was my brother that was drinking and drugging. He was as I later learned the biggest drug dealer in Loveland! My older brother was head of DEA in the neighboring town! But, because Mom loved my brother and hated me, I was the bad one! When she was done trashing my room, I'd go in, lock the door, get out my metal nut picker, and proceed to dig holes in my wrists crying to God asking Him to please make the pain stop. Why does she hate me so much? What have I done so wrong that my own mother and grandmother hated me so much? Why am I so unlovable?

Mema would come up for a week at a time. Whenever she arrived, we'd have to go and pick her up, as she didn't drive. Upon her arrival, everyone gathered around the kitchen table as she proceeded to hand out the gifts she always brought for all the kids. Not once did she give one to me. I take that back. One time, when she returned from Scotland, I was given a kilt (a Scottish skirt). She had brought back one for each of us. But, all of the other times, I'd always ask, why didn't I get one? She would respond, "You don't deserve one."

One day, I ran out to the garage crying (it was storming horribly). Mom came out and asked what was wrong. I said, "Why does Mema hate me and never give me a gift?"

She said, "Well, because you don't deserve it like she said."

I never knew what it was that I did, to be so undeserving. One time during her visit, as she was going to bed, she demanded I kissed her good night. I refused and ran away. She started yelling, "Barbara, get back here and kiss me, Right now."

I went and hid in our formal living room. She started after me yelling continuously. As she came through the living room in the dark, she ran into the coffee table, hit her knee, and started yelling at Mom about how "rotten of a kid Barbara is." Mom came after me telling me how bad I was and made me apologize and go to bed. To this day, I refuse to acknowledge that my name is "Barbara," and am in the process of having it legally changed to "Barbie." On my birth certificate, Mom put Barbara. On my social security, Dad put Barbie! All my life everyone has called me "Barbie!" In my eyes, Dad always wins!

Every summer, Bonnie and I had to go and spend a week with Mema. We dreaded and hated having to do this. Mema worked at a funeral home. She would make us, one night a week, go down where the bodies were and clean for her. Bonnie and I were terrified. Then, there'd always be the evenings when Mema was drunk, yelling, screaming, and falling down. There were many nights as a child that I remember Dad being called to go and take Mema to the hospital because of a drunken episode and she'd have serious accidents falling. I remember one time she fell down her twenty-three steps. I remember this because I would sit at our front living room window watching outside waiting for Dad's return home. On one of our "trips to Mema's, we cleaned downstairs in the funeral home, and as a reward, Bonnie and I were allowed to walk to the end of the road to the carry-out and get a Barq's Cream Soda and Rootbeer!

Barq's Rootbeer! As a reward for cleaning the funeral home for Mema, she would allow us to walk down the street and get a Barq's Rootbeer or Cream Soda!

The next day, we would ride the "People Bus" to downtown Cincinnati, and we were allowed to put a dime in the meter for our ride! I can remember how big the buildings looked, and there was this huge hole in the ground! Being from the country and so secluded, I'd never seen anything like it! It is now a very busy place, and it's called "Fountain Square!" These pictures show the old downtown, the "hole" in the ground, and the "beautiful" downtown today.

How downtown Cincinnati on our visits with Mema looked before they began digging to build Fountain Square.

The hole we saw on our visits with Mema to downtown Cincinnati where they were digging to build Fountain Square.

How Fountain Square in downtown Cincinnati looks today! I worked down there for 16 years and loved to sit at the square on lunchtime!

MY PATH OF FAITH

Recently, I was reading some journals that I'd written over the years, and I came across something I'd completely forgotten. When my oldest brother, Steve, came home from Vietnam, he came home with a woman and my parents were not too pleased with him. That relationship didn't last too long. He moved on to another woman, moving in with her and her three daughters. They didn't at first get married, and this was against everything my parents believed in. Again, "what would everyone think of them!" So they did to them what they would eventually do to me also. They disowned Steve. I was sixteen at the time and use to sneak over to see them and their girls, taking them out to see movies and to babysit.

In high school, I started running track but started having blackouts while running and at other various times. They weren't normal blackouts. I would break out in a cold sweat, my vision would go black with spots, my ears would ring and I would throw up. It would happen a lot when I moved suddenly, exercised induced, or if I'd been sleeping and was awakened suddenly. The doctors had no idea what it was and to make matters worse, I had a lump growing at the base of my skull. They decided to hospitalize me and run tests. I ended up in the hospital for over a week because, somehow, everyone forgot I was in there and just left me there. The doctors, Mom, Dad, and everyone, I was just forgotten! No tests were even run until the following week! This was only because I finally called Steve!

I told him what was going on. I told him no one was coming to see me or doing anything. He, at first, wouldn't get involved because of their situation. By the end of the week, Steve was at the hospital and had Mom, Dad, and the doctors there. He was the one that got people moving! Steve and I had talked, and we had decided that he needed to get back with Mom and Dad. I had always been the peacekeeper of the family, at all costs to myself and still am. It worked! Steve, Barb, and their family were reunited with Mom and Dad! As it turned out, I was having severe migraines and was under severe stress. The lump on my head, for lack of medical terminology, was a retarded oil gland! I was not allowed to run track anymore either.

The weirdest thing though, not long after this, Steve and Barb never talked to me again.

I'd had crushes on some boys, but none had ever liked me. At the age of sixteen, I was asked out by *the* most popular guy at the school. The football star, "the guy every girl wanted to date." I thought it was a joke. I'd never been on a date or even asked out! Then to top it off, I was even allowed to go! I was, truthfully, terrified. I had no idea what to talk to him about or what to say! I didn't really ever get to talk to people! I hung out with my horse, cats, chickens, and God! My big date night came. He took me to the drive-in to see a movie. We parked next to his friends, and he lit up something in the car that started making me lightheaded. He got out of the car and started drinking with his friends. I stayed in the car not feeling good and very uncomfortable. I finally told him I wanted to go home. I didn't like what was going on. He said he'd take me home.

On the way home, I said to him; this isn't the way home. He said I know and pulled into a parking lot of an apartment complex that was under construction. I told him to take me home. He proceeded to climb on top of me and start ripping off my clothes. I tried to stop him, yelling at him to stop. The next thing I remember is getting out of the car at my house standing at the front door with my clothes all torn up, thinking OMG, I can't let my parents see me. Mom already hates me. What will she do to me after this? I snuck in took a shower and went to bed asking God what just happened to me and why did I feel so bad and hurt so much? What did I do to deserve this? Why am I being punished? Am I what Mom says I am? What a great way to learn about sex.

I told my boss at the bakery about it the next day. She was an angel to me and helped me so much. About a month later, she asked me when my last period had been. I didn't know. I'd been in such a daze since it all happened. She said, "I think you're pregnant." So, she bought a pregnancy test for me, and I was. I was even more devastated. When she called the rapist and told him, he laughed at her. He told her I had wanted it and hung up on her. Oh, dear Lord, what did I do to make him think I wanted this nightmare? I live with it to this day. I cry over it to this day.

She was so much more than a boss. She was a friend and helped me, guiding me, and helped me to schedule and get an abortion. She too knew what Mom was like. She wanted me to have a life. She's not for this type of thing but understood the tragedy and circumstances of the time. This is something I'm not proud of, but that's what happened. I almost died from it and was sick for the next few weeks with a high fever. My parents didn't even notice. I kept asking God, "Why?" I felt like I was being punished for being such a bad person. If my own mother couldn't love me then, how could God or anyone else? Maybe Mom was right; I am a horrible person and no good. My life started spiraling downhill at this point. I started doubting, everything, even God.

The hard and sad thing with all of this is that I still think of this baby, about being raped, and not able to go to my parents. I hate myself for all of it. I know God has forgiven me, but I still don't know if I can forgive myself. I don't believe in abortion. I would never tell anyone to do it, but I do believe my friend saved my life at that time. I began at a very early age talking to my kids about sex so that we could be very open and honest, and no matter what, they could always come to me with anything and know I would always be there for them. I did things to try to get revenge on the boy who raped me that he doesn't even know that I did. They were only minor childish things. Now that I think back on them, they were not even harmful! Egging his parent's house was one! I was so full of anger and hate for him, my parents, and myself. I didn't know how to deal with any of it. I hurt myself for many years because of all this anger and hate. This was only the beginning of my wrath upon myself. The destruction of hatred of what I would do to myself over the next few years.

One day, I wanted to go with Dad to get railroad ties. Mom refused to let me go. She said I had to help her do some work. At this time, I was on Valium for depression! Dad left, and Mom lay down to take a nap! She'd lied to me again! I went and took one of my Valium (no more nut picker for me to make the pain go away). I was laying on the living room couch and thought, *I don't feel it, I'm tired of hurting*, so I went and took a couple more. About ten minutes later, I thought the same thing. Next thing I knew, I was laying on our family room couch with the neighbor doctor over me and mom was yelling, "How could you do this?"

What will people think? Dr. Dan had given me Ipecac syrup. Apparently, I'd taken all sixty of the Valium, walked outside, and fell face first into the lake. My brother, Jimmy, found me laying there face down in the lake. I was told never to tell anyone of this, so I don't embarrass my mother!

I'd started school that year as a junior, and on the first day, I saw my rapist. I went straight to the counselor. Crying to her telling her all of what had happened wanting to quit school. I just couldn't go to school seeing him every day. They immediately transferred me the next day to vocational school. Both school counselors got me into some counseling. When my parents learned I was going to counseling, they threatened to sue the schools if I continued. The fights with Mom and I were more frequent and much worse.

One day, as Mom was screaming how much she hated me and how rotten and horrible I was, I packed a suitcase and told her I was leaving. I was seventeen at the time. She said that was fine; she never wanted me anyway. I cracked. I told her that a year ago I'd been raped, had gotten pregnant from the rape, had an abortion, and had it done in her name. I was crying at this point, and then I let them know that I'd almost died from it, and they hadn't even noticed. Mom, of course, called me a liar. Dad was trying to stop us from fighting. I told her that I had the papers to prove it. Getting them out of my suitcase, I showed it to them. Her response was, "This is Wednesday, you have until Saturday to be out of our house and our lives. I never want to see you again. What will people in town think of us?"

My response, "Think of you! Fine, I'll be out of your life forever."

Dad didn't say a word. He had failed me too. He'd always said, "Your mother runs the house, I make the money."

For the first time in my life, Dad was abandoning me. I was even more devastated. I'd be completely alone in this world. All I truly had was God. Or, is He gone now too? Does He now hate me too?

Where Is God in My Path of Faith?

Brokenness opens a path for obedience. Not because it's more spiritual to be jacked up across areas of my life, but because of the humility it takes to engage in an honest relationship between the Holy Spirit and myself. It takes a lot to say, "I don't have it all together, and I'm not going to wait until I have it all together. Jesus, I need you now. Where are you? Can you please come to me now?" He has all wisdom all power. He is at peace with our humanity, with our brokenness. He comes to us in our pain, not in our pretense. He gives grace to the humble, but he resists the proud. The Holy Trinity is the only force able to transform our lives completely and for good. He is the only One who comes to us when we ask and when we don't even know, we are asking. At this time in my life, I was begging for Him. I was a terrified seventeen–year-old little country girl who didn't know a thing about life. I'd been completely sheltered all of my life. The family I grew up in was like a cult. We had our own little world that no one was allowed in and it was run by our Mom.

Scripture

> The Lord is close to the brokenhearted; He rescues those whose spirits are crushed. (Psalm 34:18, NLT)

Praise

I heard someone preach that Jesus doesn't help those who don't ask or seek Him! I don't believe this. How could anyone ever find Jesus if this were actually true? I believe He's never left me and has reached out to me, even when I couldn't ask. Thank you, Lord, for always being there, carrying me when I couldn't go on. Waiting when I was lost, hurt, and scared to think I was turning from you. Blaming you for all that was going wrong, when I was only scared and angry with myself. I didn't yet know how to live life, yet you haven't given up on me. You continue to guide me on my path.

Chapter 4

Still Running from Me, Not towards the Light

Saturday, I moved into my own apartment. I was seventeen, going to high school, working full-time, and living on my own. The apartment I rented only had sliding glass doors that faced the woods. Where I grew up, we didn't even lock our doors, let alone close them! A month to the day I'd moved out, I was sleeping, about 3:00 a.m., I awoke with a man lying naked on top of me. Then I saw another reaching for my purse on my bedroom floor. I grabbed my princess phone and began bashing the naked guy with it. I went after the other one, chasing them both out of my apartment. Then I called the police. I wasn't about to be abused and raped by another man.

When the police arrived, I described both of the males to them. They were able to lift fingerprints from everywhere in my apartment. I, for some unknown reason to me, called my mother, thinking that for once she'd be there for me! When I told her what happened, she simply stated, "You probably brought them home with you," then hung up on me! What was I thinking! Why did I do that to myself again?

When the police left, I went to my prayer corner, praying for Jesus to be with me and help me. I had a few close friends since I was still in high school who tried to be there for me when they could. I was also working full time at a company called Bionetics as a co-op student. Never being able to sleep at night, my employer was very kind, as I sometimes fell asleep at work. It was the only place I felt safe. I'd lie in bed at night with a butcher knife in on hand and mace the detective had given in the other hand or sit up waiting for their return. The apartment manager within a week moved me to a second-floor apartment in a different building thinking this might help me but to no avail. For the next few months, sleep evaded me. The two men, who had broken into my apartment, had stolen my purse. They had written and cashed checks totaling $1,200. This was very helpful in catching and convicting them. It then became a federal offense, not just an attempted rape and burglary.

I went to my apartment manager, telling her, I just couldn't stay there any longer. The police knew who the suspects were. They were already wanted and dangerous but had not been caught yet. I was a seventeen–year-old girl, very innocent, and naive child, and I was terrified. They let me out of my lease to move. Two weeks later, the building I'd been living in was burned to the ground. The detective told me the fire had started in the storage closet on the balcony of the apartment I had just vacated. The police detective told me it was a message to me from the two who had broken in. Once they were caught, it was confirmed by the one who rolled on the other to get a lesser sentence.

I'd changed jobs and found a new place. I still lived in fear wherever I went. I was suspicious of everyone and everything. I was now working as a legal assistant for an Attorney. I thought I had a promising career ahead of me. A few months later, the suspects were caught. One turned on the other for a lesser sentence, and we went to trial. I'd never had to do anything like this before; it was not easy. When I went to testify, it was "cub scout day!" I was embarrassed and horrified at having to describe what the one man did to me, let alone in front of a bunch of young boys. All I could do was pray and ask God to help me through it, also asking to let these young boys be able to comprehend what was going on and to learn from it.

The verdict/sentencing was one man served thirty years, and the one who turned on his friend received fifteen years. The whole ordeal ended in 1981. I have to tell you, every day of my life, I still look over my shoulder when I'm in public to see if one of them might be somewhere nearby. But as my life goes on, I know the One True One is always watching over me, protecting me.

These two creeps were finally put away; I was trying to get on with my life. I had a new place to live, a new job; I was away from my so-called Mom who hated me. My life had to get better now. I worked for the attorney for seven months. He'd told me that after six months he'd give me a raise if I were still working there. I'd been growing stronger with all I'd been through so; I went in to talk to him, bravely to ask for the raise:

"Mr. T, you told me that after six months, you'd give me a raise and well, (stumbling and losing my bravery) it's now been seven months, and you haven't given me the raise yet?"

He responds, "Please sit down. As you know, my wife had a hysterectomy, and she's incapacitated right now. So if you can take her place and take care of me, then I'll give you that raise."

He just smiled at me!

My mouth just dropped open, I said, "After what I just went through, and you know about it and how hard it's been for me, are you serious?"

He responds, "I have to go to court now. Just let me know in the morning."

And he left the office with me just sitting there completely shocked.

I honestly could not believe it. Maybe Mom was right! Something is wrong with me. Why is this happening to me? What am I doing to make all of this happen? I didn't say or do anything to make him think I wanted him that way. Did I?

Once I gathered myself, I went next door to the secretary at the insurance company. Telling her what had just transpired, she told me her husband was an attorney in downtown Cincinnati. She would call him and get right back with me. I went back to my office, and within ten minutes, she came in, told me to pack up my stuff. I had an interview with her husband in the morning. She was such a sweet woman. She assured me it wasn't me; he had no right to do or say what he did. Together, we prepared an email to the head of the law firm letting them know what had happened and why I was quitting so abruptly. The law firm did contact me, but they told me that I'd lied. I made it all up, and I'd better never tell anyone of this, or I would suffer dire consequences!

The next day, I went to the interview and got the job! It was the best job ever! There were four attorneys, two other legal assistants who were so wonderful and worldly; at least it seemed to me! I loved going to work and learning from all of them. I moved from the Eastside of Cincinnati to the Westside, so I could be closer to downtown Cincinnati. Working in such a big city was so new, exciting, and amazing to me coming from such a small country town where I grew up in Loveland, Ohio. The other girls in the office had fun with me as I called city streets "roads" and was told that they're called "streets;" I called expressways "highways" and was told they're called "expressways!" It was all in good fun! One day, I went out to get lunch at Wendy's and saw a man pick a sucker out of the trash and put it into his mouth. I threw up running back to the office. When I got back, devastated, I told the girls about it! They just laughed at me!

I met new friends where I lived, and we started going out to the nightclubs. Back then, we had 3.2 percent beer and, it was legal to drink at nineteen! I'd gone to some of the nightclubs to dance earlier on with some friends and remembered how great it was. For me, it was like a completely new world. Like someone took my black and white life and filled it with color! I loved dancing in the nightclubs with or without the boys who came and went. I didn't care if I dated or not. I started modeling on the runway, photo shoots, and commercials and in fashion auctions. I was having so much fun in life! Mom had told me I was too ugly to do what I dreamed of doing, which was being a model. Here I am doing it! Even more amazing to me, they seemed to love me too! I still didn't think I was pretty, but I thought it was just because I loved doing it so much it showed through me! I felt like I had the best life in my job and modeling. Even more, I actually had some friends.

But, I was still so very lonely though no one knew this. I had no family, and I'd turned away from God. I had this deep hole inside of me that I didn't know I had. I was filling it with all the wrong things. Drinking, dancing, modeling, late hours at work, buying many clothes as I'd now had collected quite a few credit cards. I'd go and buy a shirt or dress in every color and shoes to match. If my friends and I weren't out dancing and drinking or working, we were shopping. We did this for a few years.

I realized that there was something missing in my life. I was working at a different law firm, making more money; still modeling, even more at this time, but had less money and was even more unhappy. I was dating a Metro bus driver, which I'd met riding the bus to work every day. I'd sold my car to help pay my bills and started taking the bus downtown to work. I moved into a less expensive apartment, which was only across the street. Moving to run away from myself, this will become my habit as time goes on, a geographical cure! I was drinking more to fill the hole inside of me. I knew my life wasn't right. I found out that the bus driver, to whom I was engaged, was married, and that's why we couldn't get married. I broke off that engagement very quickly!

Soon afterward, I got another job at another law firm, and I started dating another man who was a very sweet boy in college. I had a dream one night that he drove my car to school, and on the bridge; he was in a car accident and damaged my car. I'd bought another car by this time! He laughed and didn't believe me, but an hour after I got to work, I received a call from him telling me he'd been in an accident, and my car had been wrecked! At this time, I realized that over the years if I told someone my dreams, they usually came true. I usually don't even remember my dreams unless this happens. I try never to tell anyone, but instead to write it down and still, this would happen. This, however, was the end of our relationship. I couldn't do relationships. I couldn't seem to stay in one place too long.

I moved down the road to yet another apartment. The next one, I didn't even unpack before I moved a month later across the street. It took me years before I realized I was running from myself. I couldn't keep a relationship because I couldn't even look at myself in the mirror. I knew God couldn't even look at me. I also changed jobs every few years, terrified that someone might get to know me, and they too would hate me as much as I hated myself. I stayed with the modeling because that wasn't a report to every day thing and more importantly, it made me feel good about myself. I felt as if, for the first time in my life, I was doing something good or rather, right.

At one point though, I do remember standing in a store getting ready to buy about nine of the same shirts in different colors. As well as other various items of clothing. I stopped. As if from deep from within my soul, I felt Him tell me, "child you cannot fill that hole with all that you are buying. Put those clothes away and come back to me." I put the clothes back on the table and walked out of the store. I went home and cut up all of my credit cards. I paid off all of the debt I had on them at the time. To this day, I've not opened another credit card or even applied for one. If I don't have cash, I don't buy it. I'd like to tell you that I became a devout good Christian girl at that time, but I wasn't ready to forgive myself or anyone else yet. I wasn't ready to love yet. However, He was getting my attention, and I knew He was still there.

Where Is God in My Path of Faith?

I may have turned from God, or thought I had. In reality, I turned from myself, from my pain. I was only running from myself. I had never learned any coping tools. I never learned how to live life on life's terms.

Scripture

> For the LORD is good. His unfailing love continues forever, and his faithfulness continues to each generation. (Psalm 10:5, NLT)

Praise

The best thing I can say is that God has never left me. He has never stopped loving me. He never stopped talking to me or calling me back to Him. Thank you, Lord, for never leaving me and for having me be still and listen to you when I did.

Chapter 5

Enjoying Life a Little Too Much and Running on Fear

I was still modeling, working at a law firm, and then started working at the newest nightclub in town, "The Glass Menagerie." I got a job there as a cocktail server. Eventually, I quit my legal assistant job because I was making more money each night as a cocktail server than I was weekly at my day job! On top of that, I had to have time for my modeling and fun! Truth be told, I just didn't have the time or energy to work that job. God had other plans for me. There were two important people that needed to be brought into the world for very important reasons.

One night, when I was off work but in the Glass Menagerie having some fun, the owner, Tommy B., introduced me to a man whom Tommy said his family owned a local restaurant in Cincinnati on the west side of town and that he helped manage it. Well, I do have to admit "Chris" was very handsome and bigger than life itself. He commanded attention wherever he went. We started dating, and I wasn't too sure at first if I liked him. He was very loud and obnoxious. For some unknown reason, I kept going out with him. However, I did keep him at arm's length. When he slept over, he had to sleep on my couch fully clothed, coat, shoes and all!

One night, as I was working, my shift was about to end. Chris, as usual, came in, but this time, he said to me, "When you get off work how would you like to go pack your bags and fly to Florida with me for a week?" Well, naïve me was completely taken aback by this! I'd always wanted to see the ocean and to fly in an airplane! He had me now!

I got off my shift; we went to my place, so I could pack and were on our way to the airport! All the while, we were drinking so much alcohol, and I wasn't too sure what I was doing anymore. As I said earlier, I was always built very small, and now I am only ninety-eight pounds, so alcohol hit me fast! I remember drinking bloody Mary's on the airplane, getting to Florida, meeting another best friend and his fiancé. Then we went to a liquor store, to buy some wine with a funny name "Matos," which I'd never heard of and headed to the beach! It was so beautiful; a full moon was bouncing off the crisp waves of the ocean. Just like in my make-believe world!

I woke up, or rather, came to with the sun shining brightly. People were all around us on the beach. Stairs to the beach were to my left, ocean straight ahead. There were people everywhere! Our swimsuits were nowhere to be found! I was actually lying naked on a public beach! What happened last night? I couldn't remember a thing. I grabbed my towel; I was so embarrassed. I don't do this kind of thing. Frantically searching, avoiding looking at people. Finally, we found our suits then we headed back to his friend's condominium.

Where Is God in My Path of Faith?

He was still talking to me. I was listening, sometimes. However, I was still running on fear and hate of myself. I knew I didn't love this man. I am seeking and continue to seek someone to love me because I believe as always that I am unlovable. I was doing things that I do not do, and I was suffering the consequences. People ask, "Why does God allow bad things to happen?" I'm learning God allows things to happen to us, or others, so that we may learn and grow closer to Him and to seek Him out. He never wants us to hurt. I do that to myself.

Scripture

> "Don't be afraid," He said, "for you are very precious to me. Peace! Be encouraged! Be strong!" As he spoke these words to me, I suddenly felt stronger and said to Him, "Please speak to me, my lord, for you have strengthened me." (Daniel 10:19, NLT)

Praise

I couldn't see your love, Lord, or love myself. I wanted to be with you in my heart but was too afraid. I see through every defeat where you were and how much you loved me. You carried me through the times I couldn't walk. You listened through my tears of heartbreak. Thank you, Lord, for allowing me to walk my own path, to learn myself, and then to always find You there.

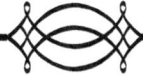

Chapter 6

God's Precious Surprise Gifts Can be a Blessing

The final result of this Florida trip; I now have a beautiful daughter, Christina Marie (known as Tina). She was born on April 18, 1986, at 11:18 p.m., 6 lbs., 7oz! She is the most precious, beautiful girl I know. Labor with Tina was long and difficult, after thirty-six hours, it ended in an emergency C-Section to save her life. When they brought her out, her father said, "She looks like a cone head." All during my labor, his brother, Mark, had sat with me while Chris and one of his drug dealers did some drugs in the room's bathroom. I'm forever grateful to Mark for being there for me. When I was seven months pregnant, Chris and I got married to provide for her. This had been a difficult pregnancy. I had toxemia and had been bedridden since I was four months pregnant. Tina was born a month early but was in perfect health! Thank you, Father! Sixteen months later, God gave us a very precious little boy as her brother, Wm. Scott (known as "Scotty").

During this time, I'd become friends again with my younger sister, Bonnie. We started hanging out and doing things together. She'd come over all the time, and she became close to my kids. One day, I set her up on a blind date with one of Chris's best friends, Jeff K. I have to clarify which best friend, "Jeff." It is because he had three of them! We all went out to dinner together, and I don't believe Bonnie and Jeff were ever separated after that! Jeff was not only a close friend of Chris's. Jeff, amongst others, was also a drinking buddy and other things to him. However, once Jeff met Bonnie, he changed. It was another reason Chris hated me. He told me that I had chased his friend away! Jeff always said Bonnie saved him! Bonnie had become very spiritual, before Jeff, and lived an amazing Christian life. Bonnie and Jeff were married and had two beautiful children, while also raising Jeff's daughter. Bonnie passed away at the age of forty-seven from ovarian cancer. I have to say they had an amazing marriage and the way they raised their children, well, I learned a lot from both of them.

My Sister Bonnie and I at her wedding. I was her maid of honor.

The night I got pregnant with Scotty, their father and I had gone out for a "big night on the town" and stayed at a Holiday Inn. What he didn't know was that I asked for this time out because it was my time to decide if I was going to stay with him or not. I knew I didn't love him. I also knew he was cheating on me. I couldn't take his drinking and drugging anymore either.

The next morning, I knew it was over, but that it would be awhile before I could leave. As we were having breakfast, I told him I was pregnant from last night. He laughed at me and said, "There's no way you can know that!" I just simply said, "Okay."

Lo and behold, I was pregnant! Scotty was born on August 27, 1987, at 8:02 a.m., 7lbs, 11oz! He is another blessing to me from God! Scotty was a planned C-Section, so he was on time! However, he was not in good health. I remember to this day laying in my bed and the doctors coming out and circling my bed. I started to cry asking what's wrong with him. They said, "He has fluid in his lungs and is in intensive care. He's hooked up to various feeding tubes and oxygen. You can go in there to visit him. When he can take a quarter ounce of formula, he can come out to you."

My OB/GYN made sure I stayed in with him for the seven days he was in there. I was never as happy as when he came out to my room and visited with me. I had Tina in with us. She loved her little brother, holding him, and kissing him! They were only sixteen months apart, but she was definitely his "big sister!"

Tina and Scotty. My daughter and oldest son.

When Tina and Scotty were one and two years old, I'd had enough of fighting with their Dad. Enough of finding the babysitter/his server/his friend's fiancés, clothes in my drawers. I was tired of being left alone all the time. His own mother told me one day when we were alone, "you need to get away from him before it's too late like it was for me."

One winter, we'd had a horrible ice storm. I was at home alone with the babies when the generator blew. We had no heat or electric for a week. His Mom made him come and get us (he'd been staying at the restaurant with his "waitress" to work so I was told!). When he came in, the babies were in my bed sleeping trying to keep warm. He held up his lighter to see us. The flint flew out of it and landed on Scotty's little arm burning a hole in his arm. He was so drunk it didn't register what he'd done. My babies and I got to his Mom's house and stayed there until the generator was repaired.

Where Is God in My Path of Faith?

I believe I was with Chris solely for my two beautiful children to be born. I truly believe that they have a greater purpose to serve in this life. What that is, I do not know. That is for them to find out and accomplish. My job with them was to protect and teach them. Not what their father knew and his morals and values but what God had taught me over the years. I was allowing Him back into my heart, and it was only because of having these two beautiful children. To me, they resembled all the love in this world. They were from God. It was my God-given duty to raise them, love them, and above all, protect them. I had to show them God's way, not mine. God was speaking to me and showing me what to do with my precious children.

Scripture

> "So if you sinful people know how to give good gifts to your children, how much more will your heavenly Father give good gifts to those who ask Him?" (Matthew 7:11, NLT)

Praise

Father, you taught me that "giving good gifts to my children" didn't mean "material gifts." You taught me this through my own, Dad. It means giving of one's self. Teaching and guiding my children and, no matter how hard it is, disciplining them. Dad was very hard on me at times, just as you can be with your children. We only do this because we want the very best for our children. Thank you for showing me this and allowing me to be the same with my children. Thank you for giving me the strength to leave Chris. Thank you for the strength to try to give Tina and Scotty a better life. Even if it meant, failing them in their eyes.

Chapter 7

Strength to Protect my Children, Standing on My Own

A short while later, I decided it was time for me to get a job. I'd been sitting on the floor crying in my kitchen (after getting the kids to bed for the night), and I realized I was sitting there drinking with a straw in a wine bottle. I got on my knees and prayed for God to help me. I was being just like my mother, and I needed to take action and change.

I found a job at a law firm as a legal assistant. I loved my new-found freedom. I had Tina and Scotty in a Christian Day Care. I was saving up to prepare for our move. Tina always tended to get ear infections, and at this particular time, she had them. I'd just bought some children's Tylenol and hadn't yet opened either bottle. They were sitting on the top of the headboard of our bed. The kids were in our bed. Chris was passed out. I'd told him to feed them, give her the Tylenol, and take them to daycare. I kept trying to call. When I finally got thru, I was talking to Tina. She's always been extremely intelligent, grown up, and wise beyond her years. They were very hungry, it was late, and she said they'd had some candy to eat from on the bed. I finally got their Dad on the line and what had happened was that the kids had opened both bottles of Tylenol and swallowed all the pills.

I was terrified and furious. I hung up and called the poison control center. They took down our phone number and called an ambulance. My kids were going to die. I met the ambulance at the hospital. Their dad showed up. Poison Control had called him. They had to pump both kid's stomachs. They wanted me to hold them down. I refused and told their Dad, "You did this to our kids, so you hold them down and watch what pain you have caused them." I cradled them and loved them as they cried. Thank You, Father, You saved them for some purpose, which You have for them.

Shortly after this, I told Chris I was leaving with the kids. We needed to split "temporarily." I knew it was the only way he'd let me go. I knew this was a day long-coming since the morning I told him I was pregnant with Scotty.

Where Is God in My Path of Faith?

God is giving me the strength to stand on my own and not be someone to take advantage of or be hurt anymore. He is saving my children for me to see what it is I need to do. He is showing me exactly what kind of father they have to make me move quickly.

Scripture

> Evil people will surely be punished, but the children of the godly will go free. (Proverbs 11:21, NLT)

Praise

Thank you, Lord, you saved my children. I will move forward quickly to do Your will. Help me to protect, teach, and guide them until they are old enough to go on their own path. Amen.

Chapter 8

Experiencing the Love of Christ

I had a great job at a law firm as a legal assistant, found an apartment, took my two babies, and moved out into a secure apartment. Time to start living again! Tina and Scotty were in daycare while I worked. At first, their Dad came to get them from me every other weekend and every other Wednesday, bringing the girlfriend with him, of course. He'd take them to the "restaurant to party with him" or to his Mom's. His Mom, Laverne, was a wonderful woman. I confided a lot in Laverne, Chris's Mom, and sought out her guidance. I talked to her and told her of my plans to leave Chris one day as we were washing dishes together in her kitchen.

As I said earlier, she told me right before I left him, that I needed to get away from him before it was too late like it had been with her and Henry (her ex-husband who did the same to her, but she had nine kids). She also told me that I would always be her daughter. She would always love me. She had a big heart full of love. Her girls and most of her boys have big hearts too. I'm not going to say anything bad or trash the family. I'm only talking about my relationship with the man I had married at the time we were married. Some people are just different when they are matched together. They are only meant to be together for a short period of time for only a certain purpose that only God has planned. It doesn't mean what either of us was, are, or will ever be this person again. It just means this is how it was.

There are no ill feelings or judgments against him or his girlfriend who is now his wife. I love both them and his entire family through Jesus' Eyes.

In fact, I've tried to contact one of his sisters, Mary, a few times because of a cruel "joke" one of their brother's girlfriends, Sherilyn, did, and I was involved. I didn't partake, but I didn't stop it either. Sherilyn and I were in "Drug Emporium" shopping, and as we checked out, there was a registration for to win two free weeks at a fitness club. She thought it would be funny to enroll Mary in the drawing as back then Mary was just a little bit heavier than we were. I don't know if Mary ever knew, but it is something that has been heavy on my heart all of these years. It has been over thirty years. For me, it has never paid off to be part of doing anything to someone else that is not nice. If I don't try to stop what is being done and allow it to happen, it is just the same as me doing it to them myself. I deeply regret doing this whether she knew about it or not. (Here's God again!)

Chris would at times bring the kids home to me and instead of ringing the bell for me to unlock the front door; he'd break in my window or break in the door. He'd have each of the kids wrapped in his arms as if they were footballs. He'd tell me that he was trying to catch me cheating on him! One day I went to pick up the kids at daycare. The director called me into her office upon my arrival. She needed to talk to me. *Oh, no, now what's wrong,* I thought. She asked me if Tina and Scotty sleep with me at night. I told her yes, I couldn't seem to get them to stay in their own beds no matter what I try.

She said I know what the problem is! I said, really, what is it? Please, tell me! She then said something that just floored me. It's amazing to me to this day, how observant our children are, even though they grow up, they may forget all of it. The director said, "Tina and Scotty, both in separate rooms with separate teachers, went to their teachers today and told them that they have to sleep with their Mommy at night in her bed to protect her from their Daddy so he can't hurt her."

MY PATH OF FAITH

I started crying and told her what he'd been doing. I was in the midst of a breakdown because of all that he'd been doing to them and me. What she told me put me over the edge. I was hurting my children. I couldn't take it anymore. What do I do? How do I do it? I don't have a clue. I took them home and called the psychiatrist I'd been seeing. I was crying and shaking uncontrollably. He wanted me to go to the hospital for a few days to get myself together, so I could help myself and I could help my kids. I had to make arrangements, so I called the only person I could trust and depend on; I called my little sister, Bonnie. She was going to take them for a few days and help me.

While in the hospital, I became a stronger Christian woman again. The psychiatrist suggested that I move across the river to keep us safe. He said there was something about moving from Cincinnati, Ohio, to Northern Kentucky. The Ohio River/Bridge that separated them made the abuser stop. I didn't know if it was true or not, but I would do anything to help us. I took my two babies, and we moved to Northern Kentucky! The visitation slowed down tremendously and then it was hardly at all. When he did pick them up, it was just to drop them off at his Mom's house. They'd come home on occasion and tell me, "Daddy had them 'drink alcohol' when he had them with him at the restaurant." The police in "his city" wouldn't do anything, nor would the judge—who was a friend of his Dad's. I just started calling the police in Kentucky as he was bringing them home, and I knew he'd been drinking. Eventually, though my kids will argue this, the visitations almost completely stopped or went to about once a month for a weekend unless his Mom or Step-Mom would want to see them.

When he picked them up, he was the "fun and party parent." I was the strict, hard, and live by the rules parent. It would take me a couple of days to get them back under control. I wanted my children to have good morals, values, and work ethics. To be raised as Christians. I really didn't have to punish them too much and what I usually did was have them put liquid soap on their own finger and eat it! I had a metal spatula that would always lie on the kitchen counter, but I never had to use it! Scotty tells everyone I beat him with it! Truth is, it was just that intimidating! I didn't have to spank them! I found a book called *How to Make Your Child Mind Without Losing Yours!* It saved my sanity! The two of them did chores, they were paid for them, and if, say, Scotty did a chore of Tina's, then when Tina was paid, she'd have to pay Scotty for that chore! They had ten chores each week, and they were paid a dime for each chore!

Scotty had such a loving heart and worshiped Tina. One time, Tina had seen a white teacup and saucer with purple violets in it and loved it. Scotty saved his money until he had enough to buy it for her and surprised her! The three of us were very close. We read books at night and played outside a lot during the day with each other and their friends. All of the neighborhood kids were always hanging out at our home. The biggest problem I had with Scotty was he started refusing to eat what I made for dinner and demanded other food. The book had taught me a few tricks! I just simply told him one night he didn't have to eat. Go ahead, go back out, and play. However, he wouldn't be allowed to eat again until the next meal, breakfast. He could have water but nothing else. He had to eat dinner when we eat and what we eat. He didn't believe me and went out to play. Tina and I ate, cleaned up the dishes, and went on with the night. Scotty came in later and was hungry, demanding to eat! He got nothing until breakfast except water! He never fussed over another meal again!

All three of my kids were great about eating vegetables and trying different foods. I always told them, your taste would change over time so just take a couple of bites. If you still don't like it, you don't have to eat it. Sometimes, they'd like it, and sometimes not! I made vegetables into sports and other fun items! Peas were baseballs. Broccoli was trees. Brussels sprouts were basketballs. Cauliflower was flowers. Carrots were good for your eyes and helped the bunnies. Fish and eggs made you smart and spinach, of course, made you strong like Popeye! The one great thing I've always had, or did have, with my kids was that we were always very open and honest with each other and talked about everything together. I might have been a very hard/strict parent, but whether they believe it or not, my heart melted inside for them and still does. They'd been through so much in their short little lives, all I wanted was for them to have fun and enjoy life.

I signed them up early in any sport that they wanted. We went to church every Sunday. I tried to play with them with or without their friends. I just wanted everything to be fun and happy for them. But, I had to teach them to be responsible and to grow up with morals, ethics, etc. I never forgot I was the parent first. It was hard, I wanted to be the "fun parent" too, but raising them as God wanted was so much more important. That was my purpose in life at that time. Not what they or I wanted. I'm so sorry if they cannot or could not understand that. Maybe someday they will. Being a parent to me is a gift of responsibility from God. It's not just a game or fun times.

When we left Ohio, we left everything. Tina and Scotty left their friends but, they did always make friends fast. I had work, but once again, I found that hole in my gut. I had my kids and work. I felt so alone in life and felt like I was such a failure. When they were gone with their dad for a weekend, I'd get some wine and beer and some Tylenol PM. I'd drink and take the Tylenol PM until I passed out, and when I came to, I do it again until Sunday morning when I'd go to church, come home, and get everything ready for their coming home and the upcoming week. I didn't know how to function anymore when I didn't have them. They were all I had now. I had no family and no friends. I didn't know how to make friends or be a friend. I had my prayer corner again, and I'd sit in it praying and crying because I was so empty, alone and scared.

Someone I knew called one night and said that an apartment building had burned down and there had been a litter of kittens. All had died except for one of them, which a firefighter had done CPR on, and it lived! Would we want her? *Yes!* Tina and Scotty called her

"Dusty" because she was reddish and kind of burnt and singed from the fire. She was a blessing to us. We bought so many toys for her, but she ended up loving to chase and fetch the rabbit feet that you could buy in the gumball machines! You could sit for hours throwing them, and she'd bring them back to you, just like a dog!

Every day, we left for the day when we'd come home, there'd be stuffed animals all over the house, and the basement door was always open, and I knew we were closing it, so I just knew one of them had opened it before we left. I always blamed Tina and Scotty for not picking up before we left, and they'd insist they did. One evening we were coming home, and as we walked in the door, Dusty was walking through the basement door carrying a stuffed animal in her mouth, and there was, of course, many others all over the living room! Tina and Scotty ran to Dusty, and we laughed so hard! We just couldn't believe it! She'd been opening the door and carrying the toys every day!

At Christmas, we'd always decorate everywhere, and I'd try to make it so much fun for them. They would be on their best behavior for Santa, though they did know the true meaning of Christmas. I tried to let them have some fantasy fun in their lives. One Christmas, they were just so ornery and over excited! I kept telling them that if they didn't start behaving Santa was going to give them a lump of coal. They didn't believe me, of course! On Christmas morning, I always let them go down first and listen while they opened their stocking stuffers. Then they'd come and "wake me up!" This Christmas, they started down the steps, halfway down they stopped! They were saying "Oh no, Santa didn't bring us anything, there are only two packages down there!"

They ran back up and got me, and I went down with them. They opened the two presents they'd received. Two tin cans full of lumps of coal! The looks on their faces were priceless! They both said that they'd better start behaving better and were sorry! I said, "Did you hear that noise in the kitchen?"

They ran in, and the food pantry door was open and in it were all of their presents! They thought that Santa had been in there listening and watching them!

They didn't know, but I had saved up for their presents all year long so that I could give them the best Christmas and see their beautiful smiles. I tried to make everything so special, memorable, and happy for them. On their birthdays, I went over and beyond because I wanted them to know, I was so grateful and happy they were born, they were my children, and I was their Mom. Nothing on this earth was more important to me. I made the other child learn to celebrate the other's birthday. To show the other the same love, and not be selfish wanting a gift too. I'd make special cakes for them with whatever they were into at the time. Tina's cakes with My Little Pony, Smurfs, Volleyball, and softball. Scotty's cakes with dinosaurs, Ninja Turtles, and baseballs. One time, I made a jungle with dinosaurs, Ninja Turtles, trees, and so much on the cake that you couldn't see the cake!

Every day when I picked them up from daycare after school, they'd always ask if we were going to stop at the wine store! When we came home, I'd pour myself a glass of wine, and cook dinner while they did homework. We'd eat dinner, do dishes, get baths, and they'd pick out their clothes for the next day. I started this early so they could start learning how to make good decisions for themselves. To learn how to be an individual and independent, not have me dictate them or control their every move. Then, we'd watch some TV together or play games. It depended on the time of year and how tired they were. I usually drank one bottle of wine at night. Then, they'd go to bed after a story and a bowl of cereal.

Scotty started to have an asthma attack every night. Eventually, we found out that he was allergic to the milk! Funny, Tina started out allergic to all milk but grew out of it. Then, Scotty grew into it as a young child! (Now as an adult, I'm the one allergic to milk!) So, no more cereal before bed for their treat anymore, and that's when we found fruit rollups! Scotty wasn't sick very often except for his asthma and allergies. Tina was the one that was the sickest. She had many ear infections, tonsillitis, and other sicknesses. Eventually, after four sets of tubes in her ears, her tonsils and adenoids were removed, and she grew out of her sickness. However, Tina, right after her last surgery of tubes, adenoids, and tonsillectomy, did get the chicken pox, and then Scotty got chicken pox! Right after that, I contracted shingles because of their chicken pox! That was a fun month!

Anyway, after they went to bed each night, I'd go to my prayer corner with my last glass of wine, I'd read scripture, pray, and just talk to God. I had no one else in the world to talk to. No one except my Father really knew just how I felt. I was terrified. How was I going to raise these two small beautiful babies on my own? I didn't know how to be a parent. How was I going to pay for everything? There'd be times that, yes, I'd eat dinner with them, but I'd eat very little and go the rest of the day and weekends without eating because I had to save money to be able to afford to pay the bills, buy food, clothe my children, and whatever else they might need. I was terrified. I had so many fears now that I had two small beautiful children that I loved with every ounce of my being.

One night after praying in my prayer corner, I got out my outfit for the next day, prepared for, and went to bed. As I lay in bed, I continued praying and talking with God. I was crying and telling Him my deepest fears. I knew He already knew, but I still talked to and told Him. I said, "Father, I'm so afraid that I can't care properly for these precious gifts you've entrusted to me. That something will happen, and I won't be around to see them graduate school. To see them get married or be a part of their lives when they're older. To see and hold their babies."

As I lay there, I felt and saw in my heart and soul, this warm, radiant, loving, bright light wrap around me. He gently lifted me up and held me with such an amazing, tender love. There are no words to explain how this *love* and *light* felt.

Then, as a Father would kiss his daughter, He kissed me on the forehead. I felt Him say, "My daughter, I love you, and everything will be all right, trust Me."

He held me a few more minutes in His amazing Light and Love. Gently, He placed me back on my bed. I then turned my head to the right, and there shining in a silhouette of Light, I saw Jesus. I cried more but, this time in love and gratitude saying, "I love you too, I trust You, Father. Thank You." I slept that night as I hadn't slept in years.

Where Is God in My Path of Faith?

I cried out to Him. I prayed and talked to Him. He came to me and assured me that it would all be okay. He is with me, and he is everything to me. He is the One in control, not me.

Scripture

> May you experience the love of Christ, though it is too great to understand fully. Then you will be made complete with all the fullness of life and power that comes from God. (Ephesians 3:19, NLT)

Praise

Thank You, Christ, for Your never-ending, amazing love. For holding me when I needed you. For reassuring me when I was in doubt and full of fear. I'm so grateful for You in my life. I knew in my heart and soul You are always there even when I was in doubt, and You still came to hold and comfort me when I needed You most. You truly are my everything. Please forgive me for all my wrongs and for running from You. I always remember this Scripture, as it is my favorite and it always brings me peace. Amen.

Chapter 9

The Devil/Evil Is Working Overtime

I started working at another law firm. Next to the attorney's building was a nursing home. The owner of the nursing home was the client of my employer (his attorney). The owner of the nursing home, Stacey, befriended me, and we went to dinner a couple of times; or he came over. and I made him dinner. That was all. There was nothing physical to our relationship. I thought he was being a "gentleman" dating me! I didn't let him meet my kids. I wouldn't do that to them. Then he started asking me to help with errands for his nursing home! Taking and dropping off packages at the airport to go to his sister nursing home in Florida! Please remember, all that I've been through even up to this time, I'm still pure at heart and very naive and believe in everyone. Still thinking everyone is good! He said he was too busy, could I do this for him. Sure, I'll help him out. This went on for about a month.

One day, he called me and asked me to meet him at a local restaurant, which I did. We had lunch, and he asked me to do another drop off for him, so I did. The next day, he called me. He told me that his "wife's" friend had seen us at the restaurant! I said, "Oh, I didn't know you were married!"

He said, "Yes and, her father is head of the Mafia up north! There are people watching you from the hotel across from where you are living. Don't answer your door or answer any questions if men in suits come asking you questions."

I said, "You're messing with me?"

He told me, "No, I took something of theirs that I can't pay back. Those packages you've been dropping off, I stole from them. I hid something in your basement, and they're going to try to get it back. Don't call me, I'll call you, I'm on the run they're after me, then hung up on me."

You want to talk about being terrified! On top of that, I went to work, and I was fired. No reason, just let go. I went home in a panic. It was Friday; the kids would be home in a couple of hours. They came home, we went to Bigg's grocery store to hang out and play, as we usually do on our Friday nights. That night when we came home, I noticed across the way on a balcony two men in suits with binoculars. I thought, I'm just imagining this, but I'll keep my eyes on them. We did our usual stuff over the weekend as I was trying to keep life looking normal for the kids. Meanwhile, I was putting out resumes looking for a new job. I had actually received an interview for Monday.

Monday, I went to the interview and landed the job at a copyright law firm. I'd be assisting the assistant! In other words, the attorney had two assistants! She was a wonderful woman and would soon become a lifesaver for the kids and me. We became friends. Over the next couple of weeks, I opened up and told her what was going on. One night, I went home after picking up the kids, and someone knocked on the door while I was cooking. I looked to see who it was. It was two men in suits! I answered it. They asked me if I knew this man, and where he had hidden what he stole. I told them I had no idea what they were talking about and closed the door. I called him. He said I told you not to answer the door or talk to them, and do not call me. I can't give them what I took. I told him, "Tell them to leave me alone, I don't know anything about what you did." He said you have what they want; they will come in and try to find it."

He hung up on me. I still didn't believe him. I thought he was making it all up. After all, it had been a few months now. We came home the next day, and my front door, the basement door, inside and outside were all open and broken into. The house was a mess. I called the police and made a report. I called my friend from work. Once the police left, "He" called me and told me they didn't find it, and that they said they'd be back. I said where is it; I will give it to them, or you give it to them.

He said, "I can't," and then hung up.

My friend came to me and helped us pack up some stuff, we took many roundabout ways to her house in Ohio, and we stayed there with her for a few weeks until I found a new place for us. As I said, she was my only friend, and I had very little money, so I moved us in my car to our new place by myself. I left a lot behind. It just didn't seem to matter; I didn't care, I was terrified for our lives. He called me a few months later and said they got what they wanted from me. They'll leave you alone. I hung up on him. That was the end of them. I honestly don't know if this ever was true or not, if it really happened to him. All I know is I had to protect my children at all costs.

About a month later, I was coming home from work and stopped at a stop light downtown Cincinnati, Ohio, and was rear-ended. I had a pretty big car, but that didn't matter. My car was totaled. I was hurt pretty bad. I was almost bedridden for a year. I had several vertebrae twisted, herniated and bulging discs, Sacroiliac Joint Dysfunction, whiplash, pretty much I couldn't walk, sit, or lay. I lost that job too! I started drinking more from the pain, was going to the chiropractor daily to keep from having back surgery. Unfortunately, my drinking took over. I made more friends in the complex we were living in, but they weren't good friends. I had to sleep on my side with pillows inserted between my legs/knees and between my arms, but never on my back. It hurt to sit, stand, or lay for any length of time. My pelvis was tilted and sideways. I'm not making any excuses for myself, but I was living in fear, pain, and most of all, emptiness. I drank to fill the hole and relieve all of the pain.

One day, I was on a "friend's balcony, thank God" it was on the first floor. Scotty was sitting on the balcony right out of my arms where I was holding him. Yes, he fell off the balcony into the lake that surrounded the apartments. This terrified me! I was losing myself and putting my children in harms way. I was having trouble walking up to the third floor, so I had to move. So, I had to get away from where I was. I was around all these people drinking so much! It had to be all of them and not me, right! (Sound familiar! God is working here, and I don't even have a clue!) This would help me! Geographical cure, again! I found us a nice duplex the next town over! The man I'd started to "kind of date" helped us move. I don't think that I really liked him, as a boyfriend, I just wanted someone to love me. Sound familiar! I'm still thinking if my own mother couldn't love me, who could. I always asked God, "What is wrong with me? Why am I so unlovable? Isn't there just one person on this earth that could love me?"

Proctor, the man I was "seeing," was not that man! He was someone God placed in my life to bring me back to God. To be on the path God wanted me on.

Where Is God in My Path of Faith?

Even though He was there, I was still running. But, I was not quite ready to be completely filled with His Holy Spirit. Still believing I was unlovable, I was still looking for love in all the wrong places. I couldn't see it, right there in front of me, in Christ alone. I didn't see all the ways God was protecting and watching over us. Do you see how much He loved and protected me?

Scripture

> O Lord, rescue me from evil people. Protect me from those who are violent. (Psalm 140:1, NLT)

Praise

Thank you, Father, for keeping all of us from harm. Thank you for helping Scotty keeping him safe from me. I'm sorry for always running and looking for love where I couldn't find it. Thank you for placing people in my life to lead me to you. Amen.

Chapter 10

Seeing the Truth in Me Through Others

It's now November of 1994, and Tina, Scotty, and I have moved into our new duplex and are all set up. My back is getting better. I have a new job working with a temporary agency to find just where I want to go. We have a yard, a garage, and I have a new car (a convertible), and we're very happy. The kids had to change schools, and they're not too happy, but it turned out to be quite a blessing. I was still "seeing" Proctor but not too much, his daughter was very "selfish" and didn't get along too well with my kids. They liked to be outside getting dirty. She liked to be inside whining to Daddy. The kids and I had another great Christmas together. They got new bikes this year! How surprised they were!

I don't know if you've noticed or not, but my family (parents, siblings), were never in our lives. After Mom and Dad threw me out, I didn't want them, and they didn't want me. My Hero, Dad, had abandoned me. And, well, mom just never wanted or loved me, she made sure my siblings hated me. To this date, they've only seen Tina one time and Scotty, never.

For New Year's, the company I was working at was having a party and Proctor was going with me. I remember going, getting there, eating and then coming home. As we pulled into the garage, Proctor told me that I was a bad parent! (He had his daughter one time a week.). I thought it was the only thing I was doing right in my life! That God was helping me to do one *good* thing in my life! How dare he judge me! He should take a look at himself! I went in and he left. I gave him a few minutes to get home, and I called him. He wouldn't answer. So, I thought I just left him a message, telling him how I thought I was a good parent. I thought that was all I'd done and gone to sleep.

The next morning, January 2, 1995, I came to on the floor lying by the phone on the kitchen floor. Back then, we had answering machines you left messages on, not cell phones! This time, he answered and not allowing me to say anything he said to me, "Wait a minute, listen to this." He played back my messages on his answering machine for me. There were about twenty messages from me telling him just what I thought of him. When the messages ended, he didn't get back on the phone he just hung up. All I could think was, oh my goodness was that really me. I sounded disgusting. I couldn't believe it was actually me on all those recordings.

On January 2, 1995, and this is God in my life. The following is what happened. After listening to myself on the messages, Tina and Scotty had gotten up, and I fixed them breakfast. After this, I walked over, picked up the phone book, looked up, and called Alcoholics Anonymous. Now, I'd never heard of this in my life before. A man answered, and I said, "Hi, (very timid and scared), my name is Barbie, and I think I have a drinking problem."

He said, "Hi, Barbie, my name is Ken, and you called the right place!"

I thought, *Oh no, not here too.*

Ken said, "Hold on, and I'll let you talk to a woman!"

A woman got on the phone, talked to me for a few minutes, and within a half hour; two women were sitting in my living room! Just the day before, I'd been peeking out my blinds in the living room and thinking, "There's a whole world out there, and I'm not a part of it!"

Now, there are two women sitting here talking to me. They only stayed for a couple of hours but that night one of them came back and took me to an AA meeting.

At this "AA" meeting, people hugged me, they were kind, loving, said they were happy I was there and seemed to mean what they said. Then, they even hugged me and told me they loved me. Yeah, right! No one loves me! I hadn't been hugged or loved all of my life and didn't know what it was like except for God's love. At that meeting, there was a man there that was dressed in dirty orange overalls; he looked like a homeless man that lived under the bridge (that was what I thought). When he talked about how he felt, not about how, what, when. or how much he drank but "how he felt inside." All I could think was "how does he know how I feel? That *is* me, exactly! I am him!" I knew without a doubt that he was describing me and how I felt inside—*empty, alone, and unloved*. This was about being an alcoholic, wasn't it? To me, it was about what wasn't inside me, God! I was seeking my God. I was trying to fill that empty hole in me again with all the wrong substitutes. Although I was praying and talking to Him, I wasn't "with him." He was with me, but I was empty and alone. I started crying that night when the first person hugged me and didn't stop for six months! I didn't know what it felt like to be touched by another person, except for my kids. I didn't know what love was either. It became a joke in AA to hug me and watch me cry!

A woman named Pam came up to me after the meeting and told me she'd temporarily sponsor me until I found someone. Okay, whatever that is! She gave me her number and told me how to start writing my "fourth step." She said I'd done *Step 1: We admitted we were powerless over alcohol—that our lives had become unmanageable. Step 2: Came to believe that a Power greater than ourselves could restore us to sanity. Step 3: Made a decision to turn our will and our lives over to the care of God, as we understood Him.* She said that I'd done these steps by admitting and coming there. Okay, I just wanted to feel God again in my heart. I did everything I was told. She gave me the "Big Book" of AA (as they call it) and told me to start reading. I did, especially since I couldn't sleep! This will put you to sleep, she said! One day, I was cleaning my basement/garage, and I found a six-pack of beer that was a special pack because it was canned with the Cincinnati Bengal's logo on them. So, I took them upstairs, stood in my kitchen and thought, I could drink one, and no one would know. After I opened one, my phone rang. I answered it. It was Pam! I asked her how she knew. She said it was God, not her! I dumped out all six cans!

When I came home every night, I couldn't fix dinner, I didn't know how without a glass of wine in my hand, so I had to ask Pam how. I'd always stop at a wine store, come home, get a glass of wine, and start cooking dinner. She said, "Pour a glass of orange juice instead!" It worked!

I was also so amazed when I didn't think about turning off the highway exit to go to the "wine store" (as the kids called it) after picking up the kids from daycare! I had called Mom and told her that I'd joined AA. She replied, "I always knew you were just like your father!" Funny, she still didn't see it in herself! You don't know until you know!

After one month sober, I'd had a horrible day; the snow was a foot deep. The kids were misbehaving. It was forty-five minutes to the meeting after work, and we stopped at Arby's for the kids' dinner. Thank goodness, I was able to take them to every meeting with me. Everyone loved them, and they behaved amazingly almost always! At the drive-thru, my convertible got stuck on the curb. I had to get out and push it myself. By the time I got to my meeting, I'd had it. I was talking to a woman telling her this; "I'm done with AA, it doesn't change anything, after this month, I'm quitting, it's too hard with work, my kids and juggling everything, it's just too much." Just then, someone walked up to me and said, "Barbie, will you chair the meeting next month?" (To chair a meeting means; you run the meeting for the month, or you are in charge of it!)

Without thinking or a second thought, I responded, "Yes!" Then I said, "Oh, darn, now I can't quit, what did I just do?" They both laughed, and the one I'd told I was quitting said, "You didn't do anything, God did!"

I was in AA for the next fifteen years. I was not only chairing but stayed very involved in many aspects and was growing closer to My Father. (God again!)

The night, I was working on **Step 4**: *Made a searching and fearless moral inventory of myself of how **I'd** harmed others.* Tina and Scotty's Dad had them for the evening. Once I started writing, I couldn't stop. I prayed first, and then it all came flooding out. By the time Chris brought them home, I was done. When I opened the door, I looked at him, though he was drunk, I didn't see the man I'd always hated. The drunken, drugged up cheating man. What I saw instead was this tornado whirling around him. The misery and turmoil in which he lived and realizing, that I too had lived in. My heart went out to him. Not in the way, a woman loves a man but the way Jesus loves us. I saw him through Jesus' eyes. All I thought was thank You, Father; I'm not living in that tornado anymore. For the first time, I prayed for him instead of hating him. I told him I was sorry how things had worked out between us; apologizing for all I had said and done to him. I told him I prayed for him for only his happiness and everything that God would ever want for him. He just looked at me funny and laughed as he did at everything, saying, "What's up with you!" Not really expecting an answer, he told the kids bye and left.

Step 5: Admitted to God, to myself, and to another human being the exact nature of my wrongs how I hurt others and what I did wrong, not what anyone did to me. I now had a permanent sponsor, Mimi, and it was time to share with her. *Step 6: I had to be entirely ready to have God remove all these defects of character.* Was I living my life for God again? *Step 7: I humbly asked God to remove my shortcomings.* I prayed for God to remove any and all of my defects, which stood in His way for Him to use me for His Good. *Step 8: Made a list of all persons I had harmed and became willing to make amends to them all.* I was willing and reluctant, as this was not going to be easy especially since I had to go and visit with my family. *Step 9: Made direct amends to such people wherever possible, except when to do so would injure them or others.* (For me, this is something I continue to do throughout my life, sometimes quickly and sometimes slowly! God never fails to show me when!)

For me, I thought to do the hardest ones first, so, I went to my parents! With Mom, of course, I couldn't do anything to make it right with her. As far as she was concerned, I had ruined her life and made her life miserable. I was her problem. I was Dad's daughter, and I was forever a horrible, unlovable person. Dad said he was proud of me and just wanted me happy. My brothers and sisters were a different story. I learned from them how Mom played us all against each other. No matter what I did, I'd never be loved by them or good enough for them. My full brother, Jimmy, he was, unfortunately, heavy into his own disease and really wanted nothing to do with me. He was always Mom's little boy and favorite. She will forever take care of him, and that's between them. I've learned though that he has now himself been sober for a few years, and I'm grateful for that.

As I'd said earlier, I'd recently read a journal off my list of amends, when I came across something I'd forgotten. When I went to Steve and Barb, they told me something that was very interesting! Apparently, they'd received a typewritten letter with my name typed at the bottom for the signature. The letter said that Barb was this horrible, terrible person. Stating Steve needed to get rid of her. Is this wording sounding familiar! They showed me the letter. I'd never seen this letter in my life. Mom used an old-fashioned typewriter to type for Dad and other documents for the greenhouse. This typewriter had very distinct typeset and character set.

I pointed this out to Steve and Barb as Steve had also used it in the past and seen Mom use it. He then did some checking and investigating of the typewriter, finding the keys and typeset did indeed match the letter they had received. Since I had been banned from Mom and Dad's, there was absolutely no way I could have typed this letter. After all, I had been the one to get Steve and Barb back with Mom and Dad! I have learned though; the "peacekeeper" is always the one who ends up burned in the end! However, I did make my amends with Steve because of my anger toward him regarding my feelings of him abandoning me regarding our dance/singing routine contest we were supposed to be in before he was drafted. He'd decided he didn't need me to dance while he sang and played the guitar. Steve thought he was good enough to win by himself without me. (This had been a duet we did for my ballet recital and we received a standing ovation!) I had bitter feelings toward him and needed to free myself.

When I went to talk to Bonnie, my little sister, it was amazing. We actually became friends. We'd hated each other all our lives, fighting with each other for Mom's love. The only daughter she really loved was Debi, our older, half-sister. Bonnie even told me she'd colored her hair every color except blonde because of her hate for me! She also asked me if I remembered the day I walked on the front porch and Mom told me she was getting rid of me! Oh, how I remembered! She told me she'd been inside the door and heard. She said she thought, *OMG, if they're going to do that to "Little Miss Goody Two Shoes," what will they do to me!* We both cried and laughed together that day. As far as I was concerned, it was one of the best days of my life! She told me about all her troubles with Jeff's daughter, Nicole. How Nicole hated her no matter what she did. (Remember, I'm the one that introduced Bonnie and Jeff on a blind date! We were kind of friends, but not much!) After this, Bonnie and I became very close. She confided a lot in me that not many knew she did. My own niece, Annie, judges me for things I say, but she doesn't know the truth about Bonnie and Nicole. Other's judge us without knowing what is true. I've learned from God not to judge anyone, only to love through Jesus' eyes. Bonnie had also learned this! It was truly a bond we shared that many don't know about us.

Where Is God in My Path of Faith?

Though, as I still see a lot of it, I walk my own path trying to find my own way. At times, though sometimes brief, I let God in. When I do, my life becomes so much better than I could imagine. I learn love, grace, and forgiveness.

This I never knew before. I learned early on as a child from Mom that I don't want to judge others because it hurts too much. I want only to love others exactly as they are. The only thing I'd not learned yet, or was learning, is how to forgive.

Scripture

> Do not judge others, and you will not be judged. Do not condemn others, or it will all come back to you. Forgive others, and you will be forgiven.
> (Luke 6:37, NLT)

Praise

Though I know I don't always get it right. Thank you, Lord, for beginning your teachings with me on how to love through Jesus' eyes. Thank you for my beautiful sister, Bonnie. Thank you for the people that were there with me in AA who taught me what I didn't learn as a child. Amen.

Chapter 11

Another Angel Is Gifted to Me

In March of 1995, friends introduced me to a man named Andy. We didn't exactly ever go out, he just kind of came over to my place and never left. He had been living in his friend's closet and well, his friend had a girlfriend, and Andy needed a new place to live. Within a month, he was completely moved in. He was very good to Tina and Scotty. He didn't have a job when he moved in. But, I did, and I supported us. He finally got a minimum wage job. I bought him clothes because he only had one shirt and pair of jeans. One time, when the kids weren't home, I came walking down the steps in one of my "modeling lingerie" outfits with heels on to try and impress Andy. He started laughing at me and said, "What the Hell is that!" At that time, I was ninety-eight pounds and in very good shape. This devastated me. Running upstairs, I took it off and threw them all away. I'd told Andy some of my past, and he liked to play on it. Again, I was feeling so ugly, worthless, and no good. Allowing him to control me and allowing myself to become his victim.

Eventually, we moved into another duplex closer to the kids' school. The duplex was much bigger, and they had their own bedrooms. We also had a backyard and a swimming pool. Their school was practically in our backyard. Eventually, Andy got a better job at Home Depot. Now, he was almost making as much as I was! I was working for Sales & Marketing at the Health Alliance in Cincinnati,

Ohio. I loved my job and felt as if I was actually doing a great job. The president and directors were actually seeking me out to do work! Then I was given an offer to work as the HR Director's Assistant at the St. Luke Hospitals in Kentucky. I was so grateful. What a fantastic opportunity it was.

As I'd said earlier, Andy was a very good father figure to Tina and Scotty for a while. Then I got pregnant and things changed drastically.

I was about five or six months along when I lost the baby. I was devastated and never wanted to have another baby. I even went to a specialist about having a hysterectomy. He said I was too young and refused to do it. I begged him telling him I never want to be pregnant again. I was so depressed from having lost this last baby. The doctor was firm and just refused. I remember leaving the hospital after the baby died and they did a D&C. As we walked out the doors, everyone was going about their day as if nothing had happened. I told Andy, it's not right, we just lost a baby, I feel like the life dropped out of me, and no one has a clue. Tina and Scotty were also very hurt over this. Life was very busy with the two of them. They were very good kids involved in school and sports. The three of us had always been very close because we'd been through so much together.

I always kept a dream book where I wrote down my dreams when I remembered them. One night I had a dream about this tiny baby boy, blonde hair, blue eyes, sitting in a pumpkin seat, wearing red bib overalls, red sneakers, and so very small but with such a twinkle in his eyes. He was so intelligent for one so young. He told me that the baby I had miscarried had been a little girl. She was with her grandma in Heaven and was okay now. I was going to have another baby. Everything would be fine. I asked him how he knew. He said that he would be the baby and all would be okay. I woke up the next morning feeling like a new person. I told my family about the dream I wrote it in my book. The following year, I got pregnant again.

The night before, we were to have the ultrasound to see if it was to be a boy or girl, I had another dream. This little tiny baby boy came to me. He had blonde hair, blue eyes. He was sitting in a pumpkin seat, wearing red bib overalls, red sneakers, and so very small, but with such a twinkle in his eyes. He was so intelligent for one so young. I told him his father wanted to call him Joe, I didn't want to. He got up from the seat, walked across a lawn, jumped up, and sat on a windowsill. I asked him, "What name would you like to be called?"

He simply stated, "Michael."

I said, "That is an awfully big name for such a little boy like you. Where did you hear of it?"

He looked at me and said, "In the book, of course!" Then he jumped down, started running off laughing, and playing as I woke up. I told my family of this dream. Tina said, "Mom, where is your dream book?"

She said, "It sounds just like the other little boy you dreamed about!"

I got my dream book out. Reading last year's dream to them, it was the exact same description! It's the same little boy!

We went to the hospital and had the ultrasound. The tech said, "I'm sorry, the baby is turned around. I can't tell the sex."

Just then, the baby turned around and waved its hands for us to see! The tech said, "Oh my, I've never seen that before and look, it's a boy!"

At that time, Andy said, "Okay, we're calling him Michael!" Tina, unfortunately, was not so happy and started crying because she wanted a little sister. As it turned out, Michael worshiped the ground that both Tina and Scotty walked on. Michael was twelve and eleven years younger than Tina and Scotty.

Andy seemed to change once Michael was born. He now had his own child, so he turned on Tina and Scotty. He didn't seem to have much use for me anymore either. Michael was also a C-Section. As it turns out, I have a problem with delivering babies. I'm unable to dilate. I was going to try with Michael, but couldn't. So, on his due date, April 7, 1998, he was taken by C-Section. Born at a whopping 4lbs, 8:30 a.m., and he was perfectly healthy, except a little jaundice! He was no bigger than a quart of oil! His Dad, when they pulled him out of me, said two things, "Look, he looks like a bullfrog," and then he looked at me and said, "I'll never look at you sexually again." Andy never looked at me sexually again! Like Tina and Scotty, I believe God put us together for Michael to be born for a greater purpose. Michael continues to walk his own Path of Faith. He has never wavered from living a life of faith.

Michael. My youngest son.

Andy started getting meaner toward us, Tina, Scotty and me. He was violent, abusive, and controlling. When Michael was one month old, I was upstairs feeding him. Andy came up screaming at me. He grabbed me with Michael in my arms throwing us across the room (Michael was the only one I was able to breastfeed). Luckily, we fell on the bed. I ran downstairs and laid Michael in the bassinet. He continued his pursuit after me, grabbing me by the neck holding me up against the sliding glass doors chocking me, with my feet dangling in the air. Tina and Scotty had run outside. Scotty called the police on him. By the time the police came, I had fingerprints on my neck. Andy was arrested, spending the night in jail. I was so scared of him as were Tina and Scotty. He'd already beaten me down verbally, emotionally, and mentally. He had threatened me so many times telling me if I ever left him that I would never see Michael again, what would happen to my kids, and he would make them hate me. My kids never knew any of this. Staying up all night in fear, knowing I should leave him; I'd already had one failed marriage, here was another. Mom was right. I am a total failure at everything. Maybe, just maybe, I could make it work. Maybe it was my fault. I can't seem to do anything right. I had to make it work and make it right for my kids; they deserve better than just me. They deserve a family. It's amazing what we victims tell ourselves. What fear we live in when we've become defeated, not realizing it ourselves. We think that we're helping those around us when we're hurting them.

Andy came home the next morning. Coming up to me, he told me, "I'll get back at you for this if it's the last thing I ever do. You'll pay for this for the rest your life. You will pay for what you did to me."

All I could think was, "What I did to you?" "How about what you did to us?" From that point on, I was just scared of him. What he would do and his threats he made to me that no one ever knew about. A month later, I came home from work. Our parking lot was full of police. The police were waiting for me! They arrested me not even telling me why! A friend came, bailed me out, taking me to a meeting. I appeared in court the next day. The Judge said, "I don't understand why you are here today or why you were arrested. This is for a bounced check from fifteen years ago. It appears that you already have paid it back when it happened. Charges are dropped, and you are free to go!"

Funny thing is I had prayed the night before I was arrested. I had said, "Father, I totally surrender to you, I give up fighting everyone and everything. You know I'm terrified of going to jail, but I'm so ready to surrender to You. To have You change me. I'm even willing to go to jail if that's what it would take."

Little did I know how literal He was taking me! My friend said to watch what you pray for! But, something in me did start to change. I stopped fighting, everything and everyone. Even Andy and he did not like that!

Where Is God in My Path of Faith?

Total surrender and stop fighting. I was terrified of my husband but not terrified of God. I prayed a total, heartfelt, surrendering prayer. My prayer was answered! My life started drastically changing!

Scripture

> I remind you to fan into flames the spiritual gift God gave you when I laid my hand on you. For God has not given us a spirit of fear and timidity, but of power, love and self-discipline. So never be ashamed to tell others about our Lord. (2 Timothy 1:6–8, NLT)

Praise

My greatest human flaw is I can be very timid and self-destructive. I am my own worst enemy. Thanks to Mom, I will hate and judge myself much worse than anyone else ever could. Thank you, Lord, for showing me how to stop fighting. How to finally, surrender at all costs, allowing me to see, you are in charge and will protect us. Amen. Thank you, Father, for these amazing souls, you've entrusted in my life. Michael doesn't know this, but he has been such a spiritual inspiration to me even before he was born. I love all three of my children with every breath I take, as you know. Michael was truly an angel sent from heaven for so many to encounter. Scotty was always our protector and Tina, God loves her, she was always our sweetheart, encourager, and she had to make sure we were happy! Oh, how I miss the beauty and gifts they brought to my life.

Chapter 12

Covered by the Blood of Jesus in the Darkest of Places

In 2000, Andy and I purchased a house in Erlanger. Just a few days after moving in Andy discovered mold lining all the walls in the basement. Within a week's time, I became very ill from the mold. The doctors, through x-rays, saw the mold growing in my lungs. We had to gut the basement and refinish it. Meanwhile, the basement continued to flood when it rained. We had a specialist come in and test the mold growing in the basement and the air. There were seventeen toxic molds growing, and sixteen of them were deadly. As time went on, I got sicker and sicker, missed a lot of work and became incoherent. I got to the point where I could barely get off the couch and was constantly having asthma attacks.

Andy was repairing the roof and other various things that the insurance company told us we had to do for them to help us. We obtained an attorney who filed suit against realtors and previous owners. They had also been sick all the time, she had a miscarriage due to toxic reasons, and even the dog had no hair on its face. After over a year of battling the mold, and me being so sick, the doctors and insurance company told Andy to get me out of there, or I would die within a month. Up to this point, he had refused to do anything or to leave. We had to leave the house with only the clothes on our backs and then buy more and throw those away. Everything was completely contaminated. After several months away from the mold, I grew better, but as a result, had COPD and all three kids had asthma. Our cat, Dusty, of fourteen years died, and the autopsy showed that her insides had crystallized from the mold. It was as if she drank anti-freeze. The attorney ended up going to prison for stealing money from his clients, and we had to file bankruptcy. We lost everything.

In 2002, I was let go from St. Luke Hospital for missing so many days from being sick due to the mold. At this point, we were living in another rental home that one of Tina's teachers from Lloyd High School in Erlanger, Kentucky, graciously extended to us. For months, every day when we came home, we would find on our front porch clothing, food, furniture, and household items, which were being provided by the high school teachers at Lloyd High School. (God again!) I was even interviewed by the Kentucky Enquired newspaper, and the article was written in the Sunday paper regarding all of this! I made sure that they focused on the generosity of the teachers and their giving and how blessed we truly were through all of it! I'd started going to church, college, and even volunteering in the church office.

A few years later, we found mold in this basement, I was sick all the time there and began sleeping all the time, freezing and lactating. When I went to the doctor, she told me that I had a pituitary tumor. I was now working full time at the church I'd been attending and had to drop out of college to support the family. Andy had been fired from his job at Home Depot for cursing out a customer. During all of this, I'd not only become close friends with my sister, Bonnie, but also with Dad. The kids and I were going to visit with Dad every Sunday. If Tina and Scotty didn't go, then it was just Michael and I. Dad became my best friend! In fact, he was even there when Michael was born. He and I talked several times a day and we talked about everything.

I loved my job at the church and thought it was my calling in life. The congregation started coming to me for everything because the pastor was never there. Eventually, his wife and I became best friends, and she confided in me about his drinking problems. She told me everything, unfortunately. The pastor started resenting me when people told him what a great job I was doing and when they came to me and not him. I was arranging funerals, weddings, and Sunday sermons, with the exception of his speeches. At times on Sunday, he would be drunk when giving his sermon. I never said anything to anyone, and Lori eventually talked to Andy about it too.

I babysat her kids while she went to Al-anon and therapy. After about eight years of running the church office, Andy and I went to take Michael to camp one weekend, and I had a few days off. When I came back, I was told that I was fired for telling of someone's tithes (which never happened, the woman he claimed I was talking about never once even gave a penny). I was brought before the committee heads of the church. It wasn't until later that I told his superiors of the pastor's drinking. After he successfully told his lie and had me fired, as they were all leaving and finished apologizing to me, he turned to me, smiled, and said, "Now take your best shot at me." Eventually, over a few years, the truth came out, and he was demoted and sent away to another, smaller congregation.

The damage was done to me, however. At this time my mentor, Pat (who was the Mother I'd never had), had died and a few months later Dad died. The job that I thought was my calling was gone. Again, I was sick from mold in the townhouse we were living in. I had my lungs scraped eight times at the Cleveland Clinic, and it continued to grow back. The doctors were baffled, told Andy, showing him each time what they removed. I was taking liquid lidocaine in my breathing treatments so that I could keep my lungs functioning. I tried to tell Andy that there was mold where we were living, but he would only yell at me telling me I was faking it. In the same week, I lost my job; my daughter left home for college, and my son left for the Marines. I went to try to buy a duplex with my inheritance money from Dad. The money was gone. Andy controlled our money. I didn't know to put it in a separate account. Yes, this is on me. Andy loved to gamble, racetrack, and lottery whatever he can.

I hadn't realized how bad it really was. Michael and I use to wait by the door every evening to see when Andy drove up what kind of mood he was in so we would know how to behave that night. He would, for no apparent reason, go into rages of anger. Hitting walls, tearing apart loaves of bread or buns, or tearing whatever he could. Our home was always full of screaming, yelling, and fighting. Michael and I "had to go to bed at 8:00 p.m. every night."

Michael slept in our bed between us. The poor child was terrified of the dark and of being in any room alone. He was always at my side holding onto me. He loved God, and we talked of Him together all the time. I took Michael to church with me, and he asked the pastor himself to be baptized at the age of four! I had to find another church for him. Michael had to know that all of this was not of God but of man.

One day, I'd finally had enough. After he left for work, I called to see if I could get assistance to be on my own. Being told as long as I was with Andy I could not. I got Michael from school, left Andy upon my Attorney's direction, and went to stay with my uncle. I was in Kroger getting food for us, but then the next thing I knew, I was drinking a margarita. I started hanging out with my cousin. He told my uncle and aunt that he loved me, and he wanted to be with me. My aunt and uncle kicked me out of their house. This was not what I had wanted, but I was not asked. My cousin was into drugs and drinking. We drank a lot together. Then one night he, his brother and his wife were doing some kind of drugs. I fell asleep on the couch. I had just saved up enough money to get an apartment and had $900 for a deposit. The next morning, my cousin was gone and so was my money. My other cousin (his brother and his wife) told me that he had stolen it from me. I told my aunt and uncle, but they said it was my problem. So, I kept working until I was able to get an apartment. Once, when Michael was visiting his dad, he called me and asked me if he could please have his last name changed to Schuchart like me. My heart ached for this little soul.

At one point, my attorney told me to get Michael from Andy and leave the city where he couldn't find him. He kept kidnapping him from me and not letting me see him, and Michael was very scared. I did as my attorney told me, but it backfired on me. Michael hated me for the longest time over this. I took him away from his Christmas play and didn't let him perform so we could run away from his dad.

Andy had always told me that if I ever left him, he'd make sure he'd take Michael from me, and he'd make him hate me. As I've said, this threat was thrown in my face daily while we were together. First, it was with my two children, then with all three of them. I lived in constant fear with him. He finally did what he'd threatened and got Michael away from me. Tina ran away from home the day before graduation to a woman's house, who used to be our next-door neighbor. Tara didn't send her home. Instead, she took her in as if she was her mother. Tina told me I couldn't go to her graduation, but I did. She wouldn't talk to me. Remember the night I cried telling my fears to Jesus of not being at my children's graduation or weddings, etc. and He held me? All of my nightmares were coming true. My children were all gone and not in a good way.

Once I got enough money saved up, I got an apartment in Florence, Kentucky, and was working various jobs, sometimes six to seven jobs at a time, to pay the bills. Truth be told, I was working so much, so I couldn't think of all of my losses, just like drinking: to feel no pain. The drinking was progressing; I had to numb myself any way I could. I was no longer casually drinking but going out, getting drunk and driving home after dancing in a nightclub. At times, I didn't remember how I got home or, my car would be messed up, and I didn't know how it got like that. This went on for a year. I made friends with my upstairs neighbor where I'd started living. At this point, I began going through the depths of hell with my drinking.

Being so depressed, alone, and scared for four days and nights, I tried to kill myself in various ways. After carefully placing pots and pans around me to collect my blood, I sliced my wrists with a butcher knife. They bled for seven hours until I couldn't get any more blood out. Then, I took three different bottles of different pain and sleeping pills and drank various kinds of alcohol. Still nothing. I walked into my kitchen to get a glass to break to use for cutting my wrists some more. However, on the way in, I slipped on some blood and being so weak, fell on the floor and broke the bottle I was carrying. While lying there, I felt myself dying and was so grateful. I actually felt myself leaving my body, and my soul felt so warm and at peace and I looked down at my cold body lying on the floor. That didn't last very long though. I heard, or rather felt, someone say my name. It wasn't being yelled out, but it was a strong, firm voice whispering it, saying; "Barbie!" It seemed that almost as quickly as I fell, I jumped up, and ran to my couch. I couldn't imagine where that voice had come from. Was I confused? Was I Delirious? It was 3:00 a.m. and no one was around outside.

I was very alone like and I knew it. But, I knew who it was. I'd heard that voice many times before. Lying down on my couch I cried myself to sleep and slept for a few hours. Waking up, I went to the store and bought a couple bottles of sleeping pills and straight edge razors. After going home, I took both bottles and commenced to try to cut again, but nothing would happen. There was no more blood, just pain. By this time, it was the fourth day. Why I can't even do this right, I kept asking myself. Then I had a great idea! Going to the kitchen, I turned on my gas in the oven. It was on for four hours. Then I heard someone in my hall saying to the maintenance guy that they, smelled gas somewhere. I thought I'd better turn it off, so they don't see how bad my apartment looks! A few hours later, I called my neighbor upstairs and told her I couldn't do it. God does not even want me! I give up. I surrender. Will you help me?

She came down to my apartment and said she couldn't believe what she saw - glass and blood everywhere, pots and pans around my couch filled with my blood. She came over and hugged me. She bandaged up my wrists then cleaned up the apartment. I wouldn't let her take me to the hospital or call the EMTs. She called the pastor of her church, and within an hour, he was there talking to me. I couldn't go to church that Sunday (it was Saturday), but went the following week. I'd lost all of my jobs at this point from not showing up. The pastor gave a sermon on how he'd once reached his depths of hell and wanted to kill himself.

Trying not to drink and going to church for a while didn't last long. Now working six jobs and again living in yet another apartment. I started running around with a woman from church. She always wanted to go out dancing, which I of course did. When we were out, I was always evangelizing and bringing men and women to church the next day! One night, when we were out at a nightclub, Sharon and her daughter left me at the club, so one of the guys I'd been dancing with offered to take me home. I lived right down the street from there, but when I came to, we were in Alexandria, Kentucky. I asked him what we were doing there, and he said you told me you live over here! I got out to pee in the woods, pulled my skirt up, and proceeded to roll head over heels down the hill, butt naked. Remembering where I lived, I finally got him to take me home. When we got there, I went in and slept alone that night! I was beginning to see what I was doing.

Sharon introduced me to her neighbor, and we became fast friends. He asked me to move in with him and rent out a room to save money. I did, of course. I put all of my stuff in a house he said he was renovating. It was the last I would ever see of all of my worldly possessions. Including pictures, all the little treasures of my kids through the years, and what was left of my dad, which had been given to me. Everything would soon be gone.

If you can imagine, my nightmare was just about to get worse, again. I had no idea he was doing drugs and with his children. He became very abusive when he was drunk/high and yelled at me all the time and told me how horrible I was, and I couldn't do anything right. One night, I had to go and pick him up from the bar, and when I was there, I'd had two beers within an hour and then went to drive him home. The Erlanger police pulled me over for my expired tags. He was falling down drunk and had been on their radar for quite a while. However, the officer said to him, "If you drive, I'll let her go." He told the officer a few choice words as he fell out of the passenger door.

So, as you might imagine, I was given a DUI. A month later, he was messed up again, which led to him punching me in the jaw, breaking my jawbone, and throwing me out into the bushes. I went out back to lie on the lounge chair to sleep and let him cool off. He, however, called the police telling them I was an intruder. They'd startled me when they came around back to me. I had an asthma attack and ran inside to get my inhaler. They were yelling at me to stop. I wouldn't because I couldn't breathe. They arrested me!

After spending a night in jail, I decided to leave living at his place the next morning and went to a women's shelter where I stayed for a couple of months. Again, I had problems there. A black woman said I made racial remarks about her, which I didn't. There had been a conversation about President Obama. I commented what others were saying of the anti-Christ and him being voted into office. Then she said that I attacked her. I've never done this in my life. I don't even know how to hit anyone! I used to have nightmares about getting into a fight and people laughing at me because I don't know how to fight! The shelter that day put up a notice that a security company was hiring for security to work at the Cincinnati Bengal's games.

The shelter said they would give anyone interested in going to the interview a bus ticket and, you could pick them up at the office. I, of course wanted a job and went to get a ticket. The personnel in the office told me I was not allowed to have a ticket, no explanation! One of the girls in the home said she had to work close by and couldn't go so she would loan me her bus pass. (God again!) One other woman and I went to the interviews, and while waiting in line to get in, the security company announced that anyone with a felony should leave because they were not eligible. The woman I was with called the shelter and told them to tell everyone else to not bother coming! She left to go back, and I stayed. As it turned out, I got a job with the company and was there for over ten years off and on. They do security for events, and it was really part-time at various events. I not only loved the jobs, but the people I worked for and with were wonderful! Thank you, God!

However, this didn't impress the "powers that may be" at the shelter!" When I returned, I was told that someone said I was doing drugs, so they had to search my belongings! And search they did. Of course, they found a "straw" in my socks and said it was my "drug paraphernalia," never mind it was one from their own kitchen and the mere fact that I had just passed a drug test for Homeland Security! They told me I had to go, and they threw me out.

I then lived in my car for the next month until my ex-roommate called the police and told them I was driving with a suspended license. (When I'd gone to court for the DUI, no one had taken away my driver's license or said I couldn't drive). I'd never been in trouble and didn't know. The Erlanger police then began a manhunt for me. I drove around terrified and like a crazy woman. I'd never done anything wrong in my life. Remember, Bonnie called me, "Little Miss Goodie Two Shoes?"

Deciding I would go to the church to see if I could get help, I turned onto a street thinking it was a shortcut. There sat an Erlanger cop at the light. We both looked at each other. Somehow, I knew I was in big trouble. Taking off up the hill, knowing he still had to go and turn around, I was thinking I'd have a big lead on him. I made it up the hill, turned down a street in a subdivision, and found this little park. I'd never been in this area before; God again. I got out of my car. Right there in the middle of a subdivision/park, I changed my shirt. I'm thinking; he won't know it's me! I'll have on a different shirt! Too many movies for me, right? Proceeding to get a blanket and my book out of my car to go and sit under a tree to read my book! Mind you, it was nine-eight degrees out. A couple of hours later, the cop pulled up next to my car. He sat there for about three hours. Then he got out, went over, and cut a big square in my rear tire. Then he left. It was shift change time. All I could think of was, "What am I going to do now? The park closes at dusk. What time is dusk? Oh, I have to pee so bad, where can I go? I can't leave?"

Here comes God again! At about 7:00 p.m., a man from the house right next to the park came out. He asked me if I was all right. I told him what was going on with me. I have to pee and move my car out of the park before dusk. By the way, when is dusk? He told me to wait a minute; he was going to get his wife. They brought me inside their home, fed me, and gave me water, and let me use the bathroom and even take a shower. They helped me get my car parked in front of their house on the road and gave me supplies for the night. Sitting with me, they began to talk with me. She had been in Ala-non for twenty-five years. He'd been sober in AA for twenty-five years! They made a plan. She would take me to a shelter in the morning. They said my car would be fine. Their kids park there for weeks at a time and never get a ticket!

The next morning, she drove me to the homeless shelter. I was admitted and stayed for a couple of months. During this time, they helped me to get a job as a chef at a local college. The couple brought my car back to me. They had replaced the tire the Erlanger cop had kindly cut a hole, and a ticket had been placed in my windshield! The couple had also paid that for me! God again. I loved working as a Chef and enjoyed the students. Cooking is something I've always enjoyed!

However, as my Path of Faith goes, again, there was more trouble. One of the women there, who hated me, and two of the other women I was hanging with, said that I had threatened her because I made a quote from the Bible about how "God takes care of us, and we don't have to fight back or get revenge."

> Do not seek revenge or bear a grudge against a fellow Israelite, but love your neighbor as yourself. I am the Lord. (Leviticus 19:18)
> For the strength of the wicked will be shattered, but the Lord takes care of the godly. (Psalm 37:17)

Once again, I was thrown out. Then the time came that I lived in my car for eight months. During this time, I worked at both being a chef and at the security company. I was so embarrassed at being homeless and tried never letting anyone know.

After a while, I slept on a woman's chair in her apartment, for a month. Oddly enough, it was the woman who had me thrown out of the shelter! God again! On the day after New Year's Day, I drank again for the first time in a while, and it was Whiskey, which is very bad for me. I woke up in the psychiatric ward. Apparently, from what I'm told, I took ninety, one hundred-milligram pills of Seroquel, which is a tranquilizer. Then I drove myself to my psychiatrist office twenty minutes away. They took one look at me and called an ambulance. Upon arrival at the ER, I died several times over the next week, was in ICU for five days. No one there knew what I'd taken or done. After that, I was in the psychiatric ward for seven days. There, I met yet another man who was in for detoxing! Since I had nowhere to go except for the drop-in shelter, he told me I could come and live with him in his four-bedroom house when I got out. He got out a few days before me. So when I was released, he came and got me; and on the way home, he stopped and got a case of beer.

He drank a lot. I had only a couple of beers because I just could not stomach living this way. As I watched him being unable to go to work or even function, I began looking for work and not drinking at all. My job living there was to buy his beer every morning at 6:00 a.m., and every night at 5:00 p.m. while keeping him and his house clean then also cooking for him. We had never had a personal relationship, but he asked me to have sex with him and his girlfriend. I couldn't do that, and they broke up shortly after anyway. She'd had enough of him. I began looking at his drinking and thinking; I don't want to be like this. I was feeling disgusted for him and his drinking. God was showing me what my life could look like if I continued down this path (again).

I went on a hunt daily for jobs and could not find anything. I'd met a man in AA who became a good friend. That's all we were. Jim was from Lima, Ohio, but he was now living in Kentucky. He was taking me to meetings, getting me out of the house, and I'd buy him food and cook him meals. He had a girlfriend that was an addict that couldn't quite get clean. He was madly in love with her. As I came to learn later, this is the type of girl he likes. After a while, he just disappeared. I got serious about my sobriety, and I never knew what happened to him.

Where Is God in My Path of Faith?

Where do I begin? He was carrying me. He was with me everywhere I was. I was preaching and evangelizing for Him even in my darkest moments. I was being thrown out of places for preaching about Him! I was always covered by the Blood of Jesus! He placed people in my life to protect me and guide me. He always had others helping. I'm meeting people now that will be of great importance in the years to come, and I have no idea He's doing it. I've lost my children, but My Father is trying not to lose His child. I should have died several times by now. I thought He didn't want me when in fact; He was saving me for His purpose. He loves me. Can you see this?

Scripture

> God the Father knew you and chose you long ago, and his Spirit has made you holy. As a result, you have obeyed him and have been cleansed by the blood of Jesus Christ. May God give you more and more grace and peace. (1 Peter 1:2, NLT)

Praise

Father, I know you chose me long ago, and Your Spirit made me holy. I did not always obey you, and yet, you kept me cleansed and covered me with the blood of Jesus Christ. You've given me more love, grace, and peace than I deserve. I pray to now always obey and serve You. Amen.

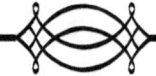

Chapter 13

Mother Mary Comes to Me Speaking Words of Wisdom

One day while driving my deathtrap car down the highway, I heard the Beatle's song, "Let It Be" with the lyrics "Speaking words of wisdom." It hit me like a lead brick that God really does love me. He loves me just as He does everyone! I'd heard so many times in church, "He knows how many hairs on are your head!" I'd always thought, maybe you, but not me! But, at this moment, He let me know, "Yes, my child, I do know how many hairs are on *your* head!" I began sobbing so hard while I was driving that I had to pull off the highway. I was dumbfounded. He really does love me! I knew it for the first time with all my heart and soul, no longer just in my head.

I'd finally had enough, again! This seems like a recording in my life, doesn't it? Finally, after this revelation, I called Nancy, a woman I knew from AA, asking for help. She said she wouldn't help but gave me someone else's phone number. She said she couldn't help either but said she'd have someone else call me. I never gave up. I wasn't going to be discouraged. I was fighting for this. Finally, I was able to go to a meeting. God was again in my life because I let him in. I would fight now to keep it this way because finally, I felt such tremendous relief. Every day for two weeks, different women picked me up taking me to meetings once or twice a day. I started praying and working the steps within the first week. I'd gone thru the steps, even doing my fourth and fifth steps. I knew from my past; I had to work the steps and do AA if I wanted to be sober. The "Old Timers" had taught me well. ("Old Timers" were those who'd been sober for over twenty years!) I knew if I wanted this to work, I had to do all that I'd been taught. "Stay close to God, live the AA Steps and go to meetings." I knew this would leave me no room for temptation.

One night, I was talking to a woman who told me about the Brighton Recovery Center ("BRC"). I was telling her, "I can't stand living where I am, doing nothing but watching him drink all day while waiting to go to meetings. My car was undrivable, and I had no money for gas." She said she was in the BRC. She told me to call them next day. I was put off by the BRC for three days. I prayed and prayed a lot! Then, they accepted me to come and live there. I thought, finally, I have someplace to live for a while and to get my life together.

While in there, after my first month, someone I was rooming with told the staff that I worked all of the steps before I came into the BRC. I was punished for this. There was a lot of mental game playing and backstabbing that went on. Being not good at this myself, I always tell the truth when asked. Somehow, as you can tell, it always gets me into trouble. I was told they didn't allow anyone to work the steps until six months in "their program," and I was going to too many meetings! However, since I was able to start going to meetings, and I was going every night. I called River Bill (a special friend of mine, as he is called in AA) who always was in my life and treated me like his daughter, as he'd done since I met him in 1995. Someone told the "powers to be" at the BRC, that I was having an affair with him! River Bill was more of a "Sponsor/Mentor/Father to me (he is over seventy years old)," and an AA icon to so many.

Once again, I was punished. When it was time for me to move up to the final phase, I was told that, instead, I had to start over because I'd worked the steps too soon and went to too many meetings! Also, she told me, I thought I was an exception! They said I could start over or leave. Yes, I am an exception I said! I will stay sober because I will work this program as the Old Timers taught me, not as people running a company say! I asked to use the phone, called River Bill, and prepared to leave. The counselor told me, "You will never stay sober." River Bill came, picked me up, and got me a hotel room for the night, alone. He then found someone to let me sleep on their couch for two weeks, and then I moved to a woman's apartment and stayed with her for a few months. Meanwhile, I got a job in a warehouse and saved, saved, saved! I finally had enough money to buy a car and move into my own apartment.

I went back working security at the Bengal's working as an officer patting down patrons as they came through the front gates for the games. I'd come in at 5:00 a.m. and leave around 8:00 or 9:00 p.m. Soon, I was asked to work security at concerts and other events. After a month with Tenable at the Bengal's, I was promoted to a supervisor! I loved not only the job but also the people I was working with. It was a part-time job for events only, and as I said earlier, I stayed with it for many years. I have to say, the people I was working with at the warehouse never believed that I was actually doing security until one night when they came to a concert where I was working. The job at the warehouse only lasted a few months. I just was not warehouse material. I truly respect anyone who does that kind of work.

While I was working and living my "new life," I was still going to meetings all the time. I'd see the counselor once in a while who said I would not stay sober out at a meeting, She'd look at me and say, "Oh, you're actually here!" About three months later, I heard, unfortunately, that she was back out doing drugs. It didn't make me feel good, my heart only hurt for her. I immediately said a prayer asking God to take care of her, blessing and protecting her.

Then God blessed me with a job at Securitas as a flex officer in October of 2011. I loved being a security officer, working so many long hours, at so many different posts (companies) and meeting so many people. I'd, many times, have people ask me what is that Light in your eyes! I'd always respond, "It's God in me!"

After three months on this job, I was given an offer to be the site supervisor at the Duke Convention Center in Cincinnati, Ohio. Well, some things had started happening. Bonnie, my sister, had been diagnosed with ovarian cancer; I was having such severe abdominal pains I could hardly stand up straight. I wasn't telling anyone, of course. I went to the doctor. She did an ultrasound and immediately called my OB/GYN with me in the office. Dr. Lang and Dr. Boury decided I'd have a CT scan done that day and see Dr. Lang the next. The results were tumors throughout my stomach, ovaries, etc. Surgery was scheduled immediately. I told work, they postponed my promotion until I could accept. I was to be out for six weeks. Surgery went perfectly. I went home after three days. Talking Dr. Lang into it, I went back to work after only two weeks. I'd made a big mistake.

After two nights working, I started bleeding internally. I was working as a flex officer at a hospital and was rushed to the ER. I was then transferred back to Dr. Lang's hospital. My family was called. They didn't know if I'd make it. I did, thank you, Father!

Where Is God in My Path of Faith?

I know when you place something on my heart. I know now I have to do what you want of me, regardless of my consequences. You would never ask of me something "we couldn't handle together." You know I have been full of shame and pride, along with fear, yet you still are working with me while I make the poor choices.

Scripture

> She is clothed with strength and dignity, and she laughs without fear of the future. (Proverbs 31:25, NLT)

Praise

Father, I know I'm more wrong than right, but I will always stand for what I believe in. For what I feel in my heart is always for the best when it comes to serving You. I can now do this because You have given me the dignity and strength with no fear. A mere human cannot hurt me if I know You are always for me. I tell others, "it is not me, it is God in me." Amen.

Chapter 14

Learning to Love through Jesus' Eyes

It is January 2012, finally wholly healed from my surgeries. I have been promoted to a site supervisor at Duke Convention Center in Downtown Cincinnati, Ohio. Before, as a flex officer, I was working 125 hours plus a week, and now I've gone to working daily at my site and still doing flex officer work. Not only did I have to schedule my officers, but I also had to work a post, relieve them for breaks, and then go to work afterward or cover for one of them if they didn't show.

In November of 2012, the area supervisor was hospitalized, and I was asked to step in and take his place along with mine! This included patrol service for the entire Cincinnati Public Schools throughout the night, various radio stations, and other companies. If we received a new company, I was the one who had to go and train the new officers. If there was a problem at a site, I had to go and fix it. Reports and timesheets for all of the employees had to be completed daily and weekly. This was also my job.

The convention center was becoming very busy. We had Lego Fest, World Choir Games, Homes & Garden, Cavalcade of Customs, Wine Tasting, and these are only a few of them. This continued until the following year in July. I was literally only getting maybe an hour of sleep a night. The General Manager of Duke Convention Center had told me and everyone else, many times, "Whatever Barbie needs, Barbie gets," and he saw to it! He was even trying to get me a raise with Securitas because he couldn't believe how little they were paying me to do two people's jobs!

Officers were calling off or just not showing up. Like always, when working with minimum wage employees, some were legitimate and some were not. You always know, who is who! One officer literally laid down at her post at the main doors of the convention center and went to sleep! I had to take over her post for the night! When someone called off, my supervisor, John S., would tell me to take the officer off the schedule for the next week. He'd tell me it was to teach them a lesson not to call off or come in late. I started telling him I would not do that, especially if I knew it was a legitimate reason. He would then tell me, if you don't take them off the schedule, then I'll take you off the schedule. I was so upset over this it was making me sick. Some of these people had young children they were supporting. What he was doing was wrong.

There was no choice as far as I was concerned. I'm a person that wrong is wrong and right is right. In July, I went to my old supervisor whom I respected, loved as a boss, and learned from his way of managing others. He was a good man and a good boss. He called me periodically to see how I was doing even after I was no longer under him. When he learned, I was driving the school patrol on less than an hour's sleep; he had told me he was going to have a meeting with his brother who is the president of our division to discuss why I was working so much with no help. While we were talking, I asked his advice on what to do with the threats my supervisor, John S., was making and what he was telling me to do. His advice to me was, "You need to call the 'anonymous hotline' and report what he is doing. What he is telling you to do is wrong and illegal." So, I did what he told me to do, not giving my name or the details except for what John S. was doing.

MY PATH OF FAITH

I'd been driving the school rounds all night then reported for duty at the Convention Center post at 5:00 a.m. for yet another of my officers who hadn't shown up for work. At 10:00 a.m., I received a phone call from the Human Resource Director, Kathryn. What she said to me was, "Barbie, we want you to come in and talk to us, so we can make things right for you. We know that it was you on the anonymous hotline giving a complaint."

I said, "It's supposed to be anonymous, how would you know it was me?"

She said, "We just do. Come talk to us."

I said, "No."

We went back and forth.

She then stated, "You have to come to the office; it is no longer a request."

The area supervisor, Mike; the one I'd been covering for while sick and who had also sexually harassed me, which I had reported, with evidence, but that too was covered up, He appeared and said, "I'm taking over your post."

I went to my office, gathered all of my stuff along with all of the copies I'd made of the "evidence," and placed into my backpack. Something told me I wouldn't be back. (God again.)

Going across the street to the office, I had that God-gut feeling something bad was about to happen. Sitting in HR, Kathryn came in with John S. and the president. They took my backpack off of my person, without permission and took everything out of it. Once they brought it back to me, I was told, "You are fired for filing a complaint on the anonymous hotline." They took my badge and escorted me out. I tried to talk to the General Manager at the Convention Center; he would not even acknowledge me! However, I do have a referral from him stating what a great supervisor and officer I am! I tried to contact Securitas's main branches at all levels; no one would even return a phone call or an email. None of my officers were even allowed to speak to me, but a few did. They told me they could lose their job if they were caught! I did have a few call me and thank me for standing up for them. Here I am again, no job and on my own. Why can't I keep my mouth shut? Why do I always have to stand up for others?

A couple of months later, September, I started working for another security company, Whalen. I drove an hour to and from work every day to be a part of starting up a warehouse for them. I'm the kind of person, if you haven't noticed, that gives everything of myself to a job. I'm very professional and take whatever I'm doing seriously. The job was great; it was boring, a long drive, but it was a job, and I always do my best and make the best of every job. About December, a woman employee in the warehouse complained, saying when I was talking to her I'd touched her! This was right after I'd busted an employee coming in with marijuana and a pipe that he'd left in the men's room. Yes, I was removed from the site! Do you notice I tend to always follow the rules at all costs to myself!

I started work at the new 21C Hotel in downtown Cincinnati. All I can say about this site is, it was "very different with very different people than I've ever known." Like always though, I gave it my all. My punishment from Whalen was "less pay and working all shifts." It was really a very easy and boring job. The hardest part was staying awake and just standing there! After a couple of weeks, it became a very, rowdy, drunken party scene. It wasn't the guests; it was the owners, management, and their employees. It's winter, but they had a bar with a hot tub on the roof, and I was embarrassed with what I had to witness on patrols up there. The general manager started hitting on me and inviting me to "see different rooms." I politely declined. He was our customer, he had a girlfriend, and this is my job. I told my boss what was going on. Could I work somewhere else? I was very uncomfortable there. My punishment for this, I was removed and given three weeks suspension with no pay. I threw a temper tantrum with my supervisor. Then I prayed, called human resources, and asked why I was being punished for what he'd done to me. The next day, I had a new assignment working at Cincinnati Bell, third shift! Now you really want to talk boring! Our job was to sit at a desk, monitor the CCTVs (the security monitors) all night. You could leave to use the bathroom, but that was it. We were told that we could watch movies, read, whatever it took to stay awake! The best thing, we had a great team.

In the midst of doing all of these jobs, I was living with a long-time friend in her house and paying her rent for a bedroom. Patty had a side job at a Clubhouse of AA and asked me if I would mind helping her with the bookkeeping. She said the last one had just up and quit on her. Later, I found out, so did the last three who worked for her. Grateful for the extra money and opportunity to serve, I accepted.

After only a couple of weeks and getting the books straightened out, I realized something wasn't right with the bookkeeping. Patty and I were working together in the office one evening, and I told her that her deposits slips were not matching the entries that were being made in the books and hadn't been for quite some time. She looked at me and said, "Just write down what I write (on the receipts, bank deposit slips)."

I said to her, "I can't do that, it's wrong."

She said, "Isn't that what friends are for, to cover for each other?"

My response, "No, it's illegal. I won't do it."

After this, I went to the head of the board and reported her. I had the evidence that this had been going on for many years. He took it to the board. There was, supposedly, an internal investigation. Needless to say, there was a lot of tension at home, and I'd already secured another apartment but had to wait a week to move in. Patty didn't yet know about this.

When we had been "friends," she'd told me about a doctor that was also a spiritual healing doctor. My sister, Bonnie, had ovarian cancer, and I recently had benign tumors and had a hysterectomy. More tumors had returned, and I was in a lot of pain. I had made an appointment with Dr. Nemeh for Bonnie and me. Bonnie backed out for reasons that she asked me never to reveal. I took three friends with me who also had health issues.

It was a healing conference that was being held at a Holiday Inn in the conference room. People would line up in a row, and Dr. Nemeh would go one by one and pray for them. I'd been in so much pain that I had to take pain pills to be able to stand up and walk. No pain pills were taken this Sunday morning. When it was our turn, we walked up and stood in the line together. Dr. Nemeh came to me and asked, "What is hurting you, my child?"

I started to explain, but he just started praying over me, and I remember hearing the singing in the background, an amazing warm light filled my body, and I went limp and went to the floor. I literally felt the light removing the sickness inside of my body and throwing it out of me. So much peace, warmth, and love was filling me as I lay there. I have no idea how long I laid there, but when the light left me, I stood up and felt no pain anymore. All I felt was peace. I walked back to my chair, sat down with my friends smiling, and told them what'd happened to me. They said they had not had an experience like the one I did. We drove back home that day.

When I went to have my ultrasound done on Wednesday, my doctor called, and said that something was wrong. I told her, "No, nothing is wrong."

She said, "Yes, you don't understand, there's nothing there anymore."

I told her, "Yes, I know!"

Then I told her what happened at the conference. She wanted to know more!

Remember, I'm working third shift, I'm not a night person! After three months, I was offered a job at an employment agency to "fix this woman's books for her." She was going under and didn't know why. She couldn't pay bills and didn't know why they were turning off the electric, phones, etc. More money, daytime hours, and office work, oh yes! After three months, I could no longer do the job. She wanted me to do illegal bookkeeping for her. She wanted me to lie to her creditors, telling me what to say when they called. She was even telling people I was her "accountant!" This couldn't be further from the truth! I refused. I even told most of them the truth, and she didn't know this. The best part of this job, I met the most Christ-filled person ever, Norine H.! She and I became close. We talked about Jesus, God, and prayed a lot together. We were a comfort to each other working there. She was the only reason I stayed as long as I did, but I had to go and did.

In this time, I had a new dentist who was great! He liked what I did for a living and was impressed with my skills, so he offered me a job! I began working for him for a few months. Our agreement had been I was to be his office manager and organize his books and office. Yes, he had been my dentist at the time! The job started out very well.

Three months after going to see Dr. Nemeh, I called and scheduled an office visit with him. His office was in Cleveland, and it was a four-hour drive, which I did alone, up and back in one day. He is the kind of doctor where he takes however much time is needed for a patient. It was a very long and full day, but worth it.

When Dr. Nemeh walked into my room, he closed the door, looked up at me, and said, "You've been to one of my healing services." (Remember, he sees thousands, if not millions of people around the world at these services.) The hairs on the back of my neck stood up! I said, "Yes, about three months ago."

Dr. Nemeh said, "I remember you."

Dr. Nemeh is such a calm and peaceful man you are immediately at ease with him. I feel a greater presence when he is around.

Dr. Nemeh began his treatment on me, electronic acupuncture, praying, and talking to me. He told me things about myself only I knew and things I didn't know. I admitted to him that my soul thirsts so much for more of God that at times I ache for it. I don't know what else to do. I read my Bible, pray, evangelize but still need and want more. He said, "total surrender." I told him that I'd done that but still need more, and I'm missing something. I have to tell you that in my life, I've always said that, "I have to *love everyone, but I don't have to like you or like what you are doing.*" At this moment, Dr. Nemeh put his arm on my shoulder, looked me straight in the eyes, and all he said was, "Love." That was it! It clicked for me!

My life changed completely at that moment. I told Dr. Nemeh, "Thank you," and then I shared what I'd just been shown by the Holy Spirit. I saw what I've been doing! If I say, I love you, but don't have to like you or like what you are doing; well then, I'm judging you! It is not my job or purpose to judge anyone! My only purpose in this world is very simple—it is to love everyone exactly as that person is and right where they are. Put simply, I now love through "Jesus's eyes," not mine! I floated home on that four-hour drive to be forever changed!

That day when I returned home, Patty had thrown all of my personal belongings out into the street and her front lawn. (She

MY PATH OF FAITH

lives in a "not so good" or safe neighborhood.) I'd been talking to my friend, Mary Anne, when I pulled up and saw what was waiting for me. Mary Anne not only came over immediately, but she also brought the police. I'd signed a lease with Patty, and she had no right to do what she did to me. She'd damaged a lot of my property, and some of it had been stolen too. The police and Mary Anne wanted me to press charges. I stood there crying. My heart hurt so much for Patty. She was this pillar of strength to so many in AA and had been sober for thirty-two years, but she too was only human. Because of the change in my heart from God's message of love to me, I looked at Mary Anne and the Police and said, "I don't want to press charges. For a woman like Patty to be doing the things she is doing must mean that her soul is in so much pain and turmoil. My heart hurts for her. I just want to pray for her and move on." Neither one knew what to say to me. Mary Anne did tell me later that she learned quite a lesson from me that day! It wasn't me; it was God in me.

While working at the dentist office, one of his assistants, that he was very close to, thought that there was more between us; *no*! So, my job took a turn. I was to travel back and forth to Lexington, Kentucky, every day to work at his wife's office! He would be there some of the time too. His wife was a dentist and a great person. However, a two and a half hour drive every day, each way, was just too much for me.

The dentist began hitting on me, and I politely refused. Then. he told me if I wanted to stay working there, I had to take a test on the teeth, placement of the teeth, etc. They gave me a chart and told me the test would be at the end of the week. If I failed, I'd lose my job! Friday came; I said to them, "I can't do this. You hired me to be an office manager and manage your books. I don't know a thing about dentistry."

His "assistant" said, "So you won't take the test?" I refused, knowing I couldn't do in one week what they all went to school for.

She told me to leave and go home. I no longer had a job. I called my friend, Mary Anne, to pick me up. Because my car was already old, and now it was in the shop broken down due to excessive driving. So, once she picked me up, we left.

The dentist called while Mary Anne was driving me home. She told me to put him on my phone speaker so she could witness the call. The call consisted more of him telling me that I was hired to "take care of his needs" while he was living away from his wife. If I did this, I could have my job back. I said, "No thank you."

When I filed for unemployment, he fought it saying I refused to do my work. I had a witness with a sworn statement of his phone call. Needless to say, I won the unemployment! While on unemployment, I searched frantically for a new job. I didn't like living off the government, not working; it made me feel useless and worthless with no purpose.

Now, I'm in a new apartment away from all the craziness, but now, I have no job! I started to get upset and scared. Then, I looked back over what had just transpired. God has a plan. I start searching for jobs on craigslist.com, putting out over five hundred resumes! God has this! I don't have to worry; He loves me and will take care of me! Wow! What a revelation for me!

Where Is God in My Path of Faith?

> Don't let evil conquer you but conquer evil by doing good. (Romans 12:21, NLT)

I jumped from job to job, whether it is my doing, theirs or yours, I don't know. What I do know is there are lessons for me in each one. You show me when something is wrong by the feeling I get in my gut and heart. I try to do what I feel is right in the eyes of Jesus and the laws of God. Sometimes, I pray first. Sometimes, I react first, and then pray! You are teaching me patience, love, grace, and understanding. Most of all, you are teaching me to love and stand up for others, to do the "Godly thing" with no concern for my own consequences.

Scripture

> Lead me by your truth and teach me, for you are the God who saves me. All day long, I put my hope in you. (Psalm 25:5, NLT)

Praise

Lord, I'm praying to You now, help me to continue being teachable, seeing your truth in others and me, regardless of concern for myself. I will give all glory to you forever and ever. Amen.

Chapter 15

Letting Go of Anger; Having a Forgiving Heart

I was picking up odd jobs, praying, meditating, reading my Bible, and living the Word of God. I hadn't felt this close to Him for a long time. There were days that I'd be in my living room praying while I was ironing for a side job. All of a sudden, I'd have an overwhelming warmth come over me, falling to my knees crying, praying, and giving thanks to the Lord. For what I was giving thanks, I had no idea, but I loved Him and was so grateful for Him in my life and knew He was taking care of me and that He was with me. I was so willing to do whatever He called me to do. My life was His. For the next three months, all my bills were met without me even worrying about anything. I didn't have a penny to my name, but when a bill was due, the money was there. I believe I was the most content, free, and at peace as I'd been in a long time.

I started seeing someone who I'd known for many years. He always had me come over to his house. He started giving me leftover food from his lunches that he had that day at work for our dinner. I was not feeling too good about him anymore. The new book series had come out, "Fifty Shades of Grey." Reading this series, unlike many people, gave me a completely new perspective on how I wanted to be treated as a woman and a person in a relationship. This man went to great lengths for the woman in the book. God was showing me that I too deserved this. I called this man, I broke it off and told him why. This was a new experience for me! I didn't just stop seeing him and ignore him, I actually told him! I tried to date someone else, but it just wasn't there for me. God had other plans for my life.

Sending out over five hundred applications and receiving many interviews, I finally found a good fit. A position for a security officer in downtown Cincinnati, Ohio, and it was for first shift! When I went on the interview, after the first ten minutes, I was told to wait a minute, and he left. Coming back with two other people and after asking a few more questions, I was asked if I'd be interested in a site manager position! Are you kidding me! Of course, I would! I had to meet with the property manager, do the testing, etc. If all went well, the job was mine. Leaving there, I do believe I floated out on angel's wings! Yes, God is most definitely with me and has a better plan for me!

Two weeks later, I attended an AA conference. On the same day, I had my interview with what would be my new property manager! Later, the property manager told me she didn't really want to interview me only because I was a woman and because of my name. She just didn't think it would be a good fit. A week after my interview with her, I was hired and working! Learning very quickly, this was a problem site. I was the security company's last chance to save this client. If I couldn't get the guards straightened out, the company was gone.

Oh, just what I love, a big challenge! I always go in acting timid, not too smart, and let the guards do their thing, so I can observe to see just what is going on and what I need to do. After this first week, I go in guns blazing and show my true colors! The way I like to manage is truth, just work together and never play any kind of mind games. What you see is what you get, this way; you know where you stand with me. I'd had too many mind games played on me over the years; I'm no good at it and won't do it to others.

Holding a meeting with all my guards, I revealed this to them and stated, "That I will not tolerate any of this from them. If there was any gossip, backstabbing, mind games, anything but working together, there would be consequences to pay, up to and including termination. Everyone will pull their weight and help each other, including me. I refuse to 'sit and manage,' I go out and 'work' just as you do." Telling them, "If you hear I said something about you, come to me because if I'm going to say something about you, I'll say it to you and you only."

This really paid off because there was, as always, one bad apple! She was saying bad things to a guard she didn't like. The guard came to me and said, "Barbie, I'm coming to you because I know you're straightforward and wouldn't talk behind my back. I wanted you to see this email that was written to me saying you said this about me." This particular guard already had a verbal and written warning. Strike three! My team knew I was a person of my word! I did fire her and the example was set!

The property manager was also learning that I was a person of my word! This is when she told me that she hadn't been too sure about hiring me but was so grateful she did. She said, "She couldn't believe how well the team worked together she said! Wow, I actually for the first time called them a team!" What an awesome compliment! Personally, I was filled with God, knowing it wasn't I, but Him, and never hesitated to let others know this! My reply would always be, "Thank you, but, it's not me, but God in me!"

One day, sadly but happily, I was walking across the street downtown to another of my sites when I had the "overwhelming warm feeling" and was told, "This is only temporary, you are here to

Robbie W. and me when we met at the conference.

re-organize, show them how to work together in Christ then turn it over to a new site manager. You will have a new mission to go to."

All I could say was, "Thank you, Lord, for this experience and Your love. I'll go wherever you send me."

At the AA conference, I'd met one of the speakers before he'd come to town, Robbie W. We'd started "seeing each other." Keeping in touch, and I went to New Jersey for a week to visit him and see what I thought about him. We were in a long distance relationship and decided I'd go to New Jersey where he lived for a visit. I say we "both" wanted to see (but really it was me, he did but I didn't know) if we wanted more out of the relationship. Somehow, I knew God was telling me there was more to this, and He was leading me. While on my first trip to New Jersey, I called my friend back home with my concerns. Something just didn't feel right about him. She told me that I was just scared, to stop it, and give him a chance. So, I did. By the end of the week, we decided I would eventually move there. When I was at the Philadelphia airport to return home, the attendant checking my bag said to me, "Schuchart, your name is 'Schuchart?' I'm from Germany, and the chocolate from Schuchart Chocolate Factory when I was a little boy was the best chocolate I've ever had in my life! I can't believe I'm talking to someone named 'Schuchart!'" The attendant hugged me; he was so excited and happy it made me feel good to know a little more about Grandpa too!

On my first visit to New Jersey, I received heartbreaking news that my sister, Bonnie, had passed away.

Robbie W. and me at the airport as I was returning home from visiting him in New Jersey where the employee told me he knew of my family's chocolate factory in Germany growing up and how much he'd loved it as a kid!

She had ovarian cancer and fought bravely for a year and a half. My son, Michael, and I had visited her at home before I'd left. We knew what was coming. While visiting, sitting, and talking with her, she looked up and said, "Okay, Dad, I hear you, I'll be there soon."

Michael and I looked at each other, and he said, "Mom, she's talking to Papa!"

Papa had passed away in 2007, and he and Bonnie hadn't spoken for a while before that. I told Michael, "Yes, I know Baby. She's going home soon, and he's waiting for her."

We both had tears in our eyes, but were so happy for her because Papa was waiting, and she would be at peace. Bonnie was the living example to so many of what a Christian, a person of God, should be. I loved her so much, we talked a lot, and no one ever knew what we meant to each other.

The following is something I wrote to Bonnie almost a month before she passed:

> You can find peace within yourself, but it can be a very lonely place too—not many will join you there or ever reach it. They will not think twice about leaving you there alone, for they will never understand. You have to know that your peace and contentment is from within, which comes from God alone.
>
> Bonnie Klumb, I know you are too out of it to understand what is going on right now, but I will be with you in heart and spirit.
>
> I do know that you have found this peace and that you are resting in the arms of God and will be with Him soon. I love you, sweet sister,

you have truly been an example for all to live by and follow. I love you and look forward to seeing you again when we meet in eternity. I love you, Bonnie, Barbie Schuchart—10/25/13

When I came home from New Jersey, Jeff, Bonnie's husband, was having a Memorial for her. I was not going to go because, honestly, I didn't want to be around my family that hated me so much. My dear friend, Mary Anne, kept pleading with me to go and said she would even go with me. Reluctantly, I gave in, and we went. When we got there, I took Mary Anne to introduce her to Mom. Mom said to me, "Oh, what are you doing here?" Not even acknowledging my friend. Mary Anne, who stuck her hand out and said I'm a good friend of Barbie's. I told Mom that I'm here for Bonnie and her family. She told me my sister, Debi, who'd not talked to Mom or Bonnie in many years, would be there soon. I said, "that's great, how's Jimmy doing?"

She reacted very defensively saying, "He's not drinking anymore and hasn't for years!"

I replied, "Okay, I was just wondering how he is because I've tried to get hold of him."

Debi and her family walked in then as if she was the queen of the ball and swept over Mom, not even saying a word to me.

Mary Anne and I then went through the procession of Bonnie's family. Afterward, I told Mary Anne to watch the video of Bonnie's life from childhood through adulthood. All my brothers, sisters, mom, dad, her family, and friends, etc. were in it. Mary Anne looked at me and said, "You're not in one of those!"

Replying, I said, "Nope, I'm the forgotten one!"

Mary Anne suggested we get a snack and drink, which we did. As we were standing there, my two brothers and sister gathered together. Mary Anne said, "Go, go over there and join them." Not wanting to, she talked me into it. As I was standing with them trying to join in their conversation, all three of them moved away from me and left me standing there alone, then Mom came over and joined them. I went back to Mary Anne who was standing with her mouth hanging open. She told me we were leaving right away. Admitting she wanted to see for herself that I was telling the truth about how they treated me and that she could not believe a family treated one of their own that way. She was hugging me as we were crying, and she was furious. She said it was a good thing I was leaving and would never see them again.

Where Is God in My Path of Faith?

God had allowed me, through his love, mercy, and grace to forgive all of them by showing me how to love through Jesus' eyes. It didn't matter to me anymore why they hate me; they are just who they are. Yes, it did still hurt, but the love of my Father is so much greater.

Scripture

> And, "don't sin by letting anger control you." Don't let the sun go down while you are still angry. (Ephesians 4:26, NLT)
>
> Therefore, accept each other just as Christ has accepted you so that God will be given glory. (Romans 15:7, NLT)

Praise

Thank you, Father, for putting people in my life who have loved me and walked with me through my Path of life. Thank you for Your love, mercy, and grace to forgive all of them by showing me "How to or, I Love You through Jesus' eyes." Amen.

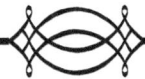

Chapter 16

An Amazing Calling for a Journey to New Jersey

At work, I gave a three-week written notice—I'd be leaving to move to New Jersey the day after Christmas 2013. No one at the company, my guards, or the property manager was happy with me. They were happy for me, but not too happy with me. No one wanted me to leave. However, after continually praying, I had my answer; it was where I was to go. Work couldn't find anyone and finally, settled on a guard working there. He was to be trained by me and then I'd leave. One day, as I was going from site to site, I stopped in at Starbucks. The

My son Michael and I right before I left to go live in New Jersey.

local news channel was there interviewing customers regarding the gun control laws. I was stopped and was interviewed at length. My uniform didn't show, and there was no mention of the company I was working for, just my personal opinion. Thinking, I'd never be on the news, and nothing would come of it, I didn't say anything! Later that night, my phone rang off the hook! Oh, yes! I was on the news, and it ran for a week several times a day! Receiving a phone call from my boss the next day, I had to report to the office. I was being put on notice because I jeopardized the company by giving my opinion on the news, and I was lucky they didn't terminate me. As it turned out, the three-week notice I gave ended a week early! I left for New Jersey Christmas Eve after going to see my sweet son, Michael, one more time.

Arriving in New Jersey at my new home to be at 1:30 a.m., I had no idea what was in store for me over the next year! However, I knew I was going where I'd been called to go. Everything started out, "Okay." After the first week, I had reorganized the tiny apartment. The area around us had flooded and remained stagnant, so I was getting very sick from the mold with my allergies. Robbie was working and gone almost all of the time. He worked as a used car salesperson for the area Ford Dealer. While I was settling in, I was learning some of the discrepancies regarding Robbie and what he was stealing from his employer. Our toilet paper was coming from there, and I told him to stop. I was not a thief and refused to participate. He responded that it was okay, they were allowed. I still said, "No more."

After a couple of months of living with him, we were fighting excessively, and most of it was due to these discrepancies. One night, we are at an AA meeting, and he was sitting next to me, as always, and when we posed for a picture, which was all the time because as I said, he posted our life on Facebook. He always had a certain pose that we had to do. I'd have to place my hand over his heart, stand sideways looking at him adoringly. I wasn't worshiping him like he wanted me to, like so many others in the world did. He was only human and living a big lie. It was just that no one knew the "real person," and he was a very different person in public. (I see now on FB, he still carries on that pose!) Anyway, as I was sitting there, I was looking across the room, everything became silent and still to me, and I had the "warm, bright light feeling" come over me. I heard, or rather, felt the message of the Spirit tell me, "You are not here to be with this man. You are here for a greater purpose. More will be revealed. Trust in the Lord and do what is right in Jesus' eyes." Then the feeling was gone, and I was back in the room. I knew why I was there. I didn't want to be, but I had to do what I was told to do.

In February, Robbie's mom and sister had told me to hide what money I'd brought with me, or I'd have nothing. He made a lot of money but had nothing. Robbie's mom agreed to hold on to my money for me. I had a plan, but couldn't put it into place until March. He'd already spent a few thousand dollars of mine, and I couldn't afford to lose more. We moved into a rental house that was much bigger, and I decorated it to be a nice, comfortable home. He brought home some furniture that he told me his work gave him. Later though, I found out he went into the attic of the Ford Company and helped himself, along with office supplies, and whatever else he wanted. My car had died, so I traded it in for another one, which he sold me. The battery was always dead. Instead of getting a new battery, he took the dealerships portable battery charger, telling me they said we could borrow it.

Robbie would do little things like call me and tell me to have his bath drawn for him when he got home. I felt more like his servant than I did his girlfriend. He was a circuit speaker for AA, so we had to travel places for him to talk. One time, we were driving three hours away and along the way he was screaming at me, for what, I don't remember. But at one point, he opened my door as he was driving at 65mph and tried to throw me out the door. I think he forgot I'd been in security for several years and could defend myself! We made it to the meeting, and afterward, he told me he would never bring me again because of being afraid I would stand up and tell everyone what kind of person he really was.

In March 2014, I started Phlebotomy school. I would graduate in May 2014. My plan was to get a job and move out. However, I was having medical issues. My pituitary tumor was getting worse. I had to have another MRI to see what was going on. The day I was to get the results, I asked Robbie if he would please go with me. His response, "Oh, I can't. I have to go down to the beach to sit and meditate. My wellbeing is more important." That was the end breaker for me. I was done. After getting my results, I went to his job to tell him. He met me in the parking lot asking, "Why are you here, what do you want?" I told him the results, explaining I now have two tumors and lesions on my brain. He replied, "What does that have to do with me? I can't do anything about it. I'm too important here at work, and the people in AA need me!"

I said, "How about being there for me?"

He said, "Oh, I can't do that. All these other people need me. Don't you know how important I am?"

What could I say? I just drove away, went home, and called a friend.

Within twenty minutes, there were four women in my home packing up things for me to leave. That night, he called me asking where I was. He thought I would be there when he got home with a bath drawn for him. I hung up the phone. Two days later, my friends helped me to move out, and a beautiful soul friend, Jen, let me stay with her while I finished school. Jen showed me a world and friends I'd never known existed. I'm so grateful for her and her love. We laughed, cried, and had fun. I graduated and became a Phlebotomy Tech on May 3, though I did not get a job in this field!

My Phlebotomy class on our last day.

The Spirit filled me again and let me know what else I had to do. I had posted on Facebook that this "relationship" had been a lie and that God was taking care of me. I had so many women call or message me about their experiences with him, how he'd done similar things to them. I had so many people following me, talking to me every day, and all I'd post is scripture every day and say how awesome God is. So many people started believing again in the Lord and the best part, not that I take credit, is that they would say it was because of what I went through and how I walked through it in the Lord. I'd tell them, "It's not me, it's God in me." Always give all the glory to God. I had one more step to do. I wrote the owner an email telling him of everything that had been stolen by Robbie from them. I told him I still have their portable battery charger he stole. Could they please just replace my battery instead? I didn't want their portable battery charger. He called me and said they'd replace the battery.

I took their charger back and received a new battery. I, also, in the email, let him know that when Robbie sold a car, instead of giving the customers their ticket for a full tank of gas, he'd keep those tickets, and use them to fill his own tank. The owner thanked me for letting him know what had been going on. Robbie had told me, "I'm Robbie W.; I can do whatever I want. They need me and will give me anything I want!"

I told him, "Stealing is stealing."

It was the tourist season in Wildwood, New Jersey. I've never been around a tourist area, or at least living in one! In the wintertime, there aren't even traffic lights, the police will clean the snow off your driveway, but there are only, maybe, two police officers in the entire town! You can walk down the middle of the seven-mile street across the entire island and not come across a car! Come Memorial Day, you are lucky to walk across the street when the street light tells you it's okay! One would think that the island might sink, there are so many people that come to visit! The Islanders work around the clock from Memorial Day until Labor Day. Then they live on unemployment throughout the winter! It was the craziest thing I've lived through but, very exciting!

A good friend told me about a position as a clerk at a hotel. I went to interview for it and was hired on the spot as the hotel manager! I've been in management a lot over the years, but a hotel! The property manager took me to the hotel, showed me around, introduced me to the owner, the clerk who was working, and told me I'd be living there. The apartment was connected to the office. Go home, get my stuff, and I'd start Wednesday, it was Monday. The last two women who had been running it were sisters. One of them, I was told, was being yelled at by the owner by the pool, and she had a stroke. That's why there is an opening. I didn't witness this; it's what I was told. The owner, Tim P., was very good to me. That evening, however, the clerk called me and said I had to start then. There was no one to cover. I gathered all of my belongings and moved in!

Where Is God in My Path of Faith?

Again, I listened to the Spirit calling me and leading me. I didn't want to. I didn't want to leave Michael or the wonderful job I'd been blessed with. I didn't want to stay with Robbie or tell on him, but I obeyed and did what I was told. I questioned myself a lot, thinking I was making it all up in my mind. But when praying, reading the Bible, and then talking to those I trust, I knew I wasn't. I cannot live a lie or with someone who steals.

When I was four years old, Mom took me to the Dime Store in town; we were always allowed to "get any item we wanted"—*when the owner told us*. This particular time, he didn't. I took a pencil. We went to the car after Mom was done with her purchase. Mom looked over at me and asked, "Where'd you get that pencil?"

I said, "In the store."

She exclaimed, "You are a thief! You stole that! You march right back in there, tell him you stole from him and give it back."

I remember to this day, telling that man I stole a pencil from him. How humiliated I felt. I've never stolen anything, not even a pen from work. I actually take my own pens to work!

Scripture

> Do **not steal**. Do **not deceive** or **cheat** one another. (Leviticus 19:11, NLT)

Praise

I am walking His Path and fulfilling His Plan. I know that no matter what is done to me here, He has me and protects me from those who are harming me, if I love them through Him, He will be their judge. I pray to have a joyful heart of gratitude, love, and prayer! Thank you, Lord, for showing me Your ways long before I knew You were. Thank you for always showing me right from wrong in Your truth.

Chapter 17

Serving God's Children from around the World

Working at the Dolphin Inn, Wildwood, New Jersey, oh what fun, aggravation, and learning! I loved this job, as much as I hated it. I would still be working there if my living area hadn't been overcome with mold. All the people coming through there that I'd get to meet and know. Working for Tim P. was such a pleasure, but the long hours of an entire week, except for four hours, was just too much. The Property Management Company just somehow never had anyone to relieve me. I was told by my friend

The Dolphin Inn. The hotel on the Jersey shore I managed for the summer. This was the view from my office/apartment!

at another hotel that the other women hated me because I was making the Hotel such a success after replacing the two women. Everyone thought I'd fail! One of the other clerks thought she should've gotten the position but didn't have the experience. Isn't that how the story always goes! There were times I'd cry myself to sleep. I was so

MY PATH OF FAITH

exhausted, scared and alone. When I was able, I'd read my Bible, and I always talked about Christ to the guests!

Meeting so many wonderful people from around the world was the most amazing thing I'd ever done. Tim, the owner, talked to me about buying and opening another hotel across the street and asking me to manage it. I joked with him saying you'll have to buy me a pair of roller skates to keep up! I was going to spend the winter there and work calling guests to return the next season. Tim said he wouldn't have the management company the following year if I'd stay on with him. I could very easily have handled the stress of this job if I would have had the help that I needed and the mold remediated. I know I'm a workaholic, so work doesn't scare me. However, too much of anything is never a good thing! I'd walk around at night to check and make sure everyone was safe and think of how blessed I was when I'd look at the view.

Working with people, fixing problems, and helping to solve the guest's issues was some of my favorite parts of the job! Taking care of and helping people! I guess that falls under "people pleasing!" When, after a week, guests were calling to make reservations because they heard about this "new great manager, Barbie," I was stunned, to say the least! I started asking, "Where did you hear about me," I've only been here a week!" It was the guests who taught me about managing a hotel and how to treat them.

There were some weekends when the entire hotel would be rented out to groups, and that was really a lot of fun! One of my most amazing groups was the Trenton Lodge Elks! I still think of them all the time and would love to see them. Afterwards, one of the wives actually sent me the book, *Jesus Calling*, which I still read every day!

Dolphin Inn Trenton Lodge Elks. One of the groups that stayed the weekend at the hotel who were amazingly kind to me even talking about God with me!

Many of the guests would bring me dinner. I felt like I had constant family staying with me and that is how I treated them. As I got sicker from the mold, as always, I started feeling more emotional and more alone. One day, Tim walked into the office, I stood up, and passed out. When I came to, and he asked me what was wrong, I told him it was the mold in my room, which was next to the office. I'd been telling him and the property management company about it. They'd told me when they hired me it would get fixed. I'd told everyone I'm deadly allergic to it. My son was coming in a couple of days; I had another neurology appointment the day he was coming, and then I'd pick him up.

The day of my neurology appointment, I was told there was no one to cover for me to leave. I said, "Too bad, I'm leaving here in a half hour."

They found someone to cover! My neurologist was to give me my MRI results. He said that if I didn't make a drastic life change, I was going to have a stroke and die. He showed me the white spots all over in my head. I left there, went, and picked Michael up at the Trenton International Airport. His flight was delayed due to storms and only one airplane flies in and out of this tiny airport!

When I finally picked Michael up, and we were heading back to the hotel, I told him what the doctor said. Michael said, "Mom, you've got to quit your job and come home with me. I'm going to be a senior and then off to college. I want you home with me. I don't want anything to happen to you."

The decision was made. The next morning, I called Tim and the management company telling them what the doctor said and my decision to quit. Tim said he'd fix the mold problem. He moved us to another room. Offered me more money and asked me if I would please stay. My decision was made. Tim allowed Michael and me to stay in a room for a week at no charge. He is really a wonderful man. At the end of the week, we went to his other hotel to talk to him and thank him. I really hated leaving him

Michael and I had such a wonderful week together, seeing and doing things I'd not been able to do the entire year I'd been in New Jersey! Michael, thank you for this special time together. We took a few days driving home and spending a night at another hotel along the way. Michael loved driving, so he drove most of the way home! In fact, he had his first accident in New Jersey (a little fender bender.) On our drive home, when I drove, I got a ticket! When we returned to Kentucky, I had a very good friend that was going to allow me to stay with him for a while until I got a job and a place to stay. There's God again, always taking care of me!

Where Is God in My Path of Faith?

Where is God in my life here! I don't know where to begin! I see him everywhere! For me, it's more like, where isn't He in my life! He provided me with such an amazing opportunity to meet people and to give Him praise and talk to others about Him! Then at just the right time, Michael shows up and brings me home! I always say Michael is my special angel from heaven! He has believed since before he was born and like me, he's had God in his heart his entire life. He, too, has that innocent faith and love for God that he just is.

Scripture

> This I declare about the Lord: He alone is my refuge, my place of safety; he is my God, and I trust him. (Psalm 91:2, NLT)

Praise

Thank you, Father, for so many wonderful opportunities and people you have placed in my life, which have helped me to grow spiritually. Thank you for this amazing spirit-filled child you have graced me with. Thank you for opening my eyes to see the truth and light. Amen

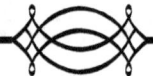

Chapter 18

Starting Over in Kentucky, Again Heading toward My Ending

So here I am, back in Kentucky, living with a friend, no job, but at least I've saved up some money! It's time to take the exam to be a certified phlebotomist! Hitting the books for a week, then I take the test and pass! Getting a job as a CPT is not as easy as I thought it would be. Every job I applied for wanted you to have one to two years' experience! How does one get the experience if I can't get a job? My friend is asking me how much longer I'll be living there, so I know my time is limited. I'm talking to close friends, and someone offered for me to come and live with her family until I get on my feet. I know this is all a God thing. I've never had to "live with anyone" in my life. I've always taken care of myself, I'm feeling so dependent on others, and I don't know how to deal with this. My friend, Marty, whose family I am now living with, is such a wonderful woman. She is so kindhearted and loving; she makes me feel as if I am part of their family.

    I start, again, putting out resumes for all types of jobs, and I started back working, part-time in security. Finally, I was getting interviews, and on this particular day, was heading across town, fifty-five minutes to a job interview at a police station. For me, this would be the dream job! When I arrive at the interview, the person at the desk informed me that the captain was not in that day but would be tomorrow for my interview. I was a day early! She laughed and said she wouldn't tell him but come back tomorrow.

Before I headed back home, I posted on Facebook, how I'd been so anxious for the job that I showed up a day early! Now, at this point, please remember that on Facebook, I have thousands of followers. A man from Cincinnati had been texting me, trying to call me, and I only spoke to him one time. He wanted to date, and I was not interested in dating anyone. As I was driving home, my phone rang, and I answered it (with my Bluetooth) without looking at who it was. It was Bill H. He was joking with me about the interview. He then asked me about my work history. After we talked for a few minutes, he stated that he was looking for an Office Manager in this Law Office/Accounting Office and wanted to know if I'd be interested. We set up an interview that afternoon with him and his associates. As you can imagine, I was hired and started the next day.

As it turned out, I wasn't only the office manager, but also the admin assistant for three attorneys and three accountants, as well as, for Bill H. I was in charge of taking care of the office and whatever was needed, but not exactly the "office manager." I've been in management most of my career and what he had me doing was not office management! I'm not going to say much about this job; most of the people I worked for and with were great people and felt the way I did about working there. You really could not do anything right and would be told about it in front of whoever was there at the moment. Even if it was not your mistake and everyone knew it, it was still your fault. I would be given impossible tasks with no direction and then yelled at for not doing it right. The job also included taking him to, doctor appointments, surgery, and other requests. I was told to work overtime to get work done and do whatever it took. He approved my time, and in the end, said he had no idea I was working overtime so much!

During this time, I decided maybe I wanted to date! I went on a dating site (Cupid) on a Friday night, and by Saturday morning was trying to cancel my app on the site! I'd received over four hundred emails/requests, and I was so overwhelmed by it all I wanted off the site. At the last moment, I received an email from someone that actually seemed interesting. I responded, and we had a dinner date that night. We met at Olive Garden and had dinner. Scot Kenkel was very funny, witty, charming, and delightful. I really liked him. We set another date for Sunday during the day. Sunday was an errand day, and we had a lot of fun. He even met my friends I was living with. He came over a few times during the week, or I went to his house. He called me every morning on my way to work, and a few times he even surprised me by bringing me lunch at work!

I thought could my life get any better! I have a good paying job (not the best in the world but okay.) I have a great boyfriend, great friends, and beautiful children! Thank you for all of your blessings, Father! Little did I know what was yet to come!

After only a few weeks of dating, Scot told me he was too busy to keep driving forty-five minutes to see me. He had another house that was only fifteen minutes away from where he lived, and I could live there. I'd spent the night with him a couple of times, but our relationship was still on a "pure level." I couldn't go any further yet. I talked to my friends about his offer and decided to go for it. Once I was moved into the house, I pretty much never lived there. Then to my surprise, he told me he couldn't introduce me to his family just yet, he had to keep me a secret for a while!

I'd been living there for about five months and was not myself. My memory was becoming very bad, as was my asthma. Something just wasn't right. Then his basement began backing up with sewage at least once a week. I kept getting sicker, and my doctor was sending me to a specialist for early Alzheimer. I told Bill H., my boss, all of this while sitting at a doctor's office waiting for him to have surgery. Bill stated, "We'll do whatever we can to help you. Don't worry about a thing." The next day I was terminated, he said for working overtime without permission!

MY PATH OF FAITH

I started to manage Scot's apartment building's (Far Hills). There were twenty-four of them, and they were in very sad condition. They were low income with, well, not the best of tenants paying $450 a month, if they paid at all. I did everything at the apartments from evicting, cleaning, flipping, and renting. He went to court when we needed to evict someone. I attended with him, sometimes. I became so sick that I had an angiogram done because the pulmonary doctor while doing a test on me, found my oxygen dropping to below fifty. When they first did an ultrasound, they discovered two holes in my heart, which required the angiogram. The result from this is I have congenital heart disease, and my oxygen flows the opposite way! However, that's not what my problem was! I was put on oxygen 24/7. I absolutely hated this. Scot made fun of me and actually wouldn't take me places. It was hard for me to get around and he wanted to have fun, so he would leave me behind!

As it turned out, I went and bought mold-testing kits. His house was filled with dangerous molds. Here is what grew in the samples from the basement, first and second floors of his house. He told me it was nothing, but the reports came back saying something different.

The mold that was growing in the house I was living in with Scot that made me so ill I had to be put on oxygen.

He finally called in a professional to do the testing, and he also said it was a very dangerous environment. It would take about a week to eliminate what was there and about $8,000.00. Well, needless to say, Scot was not doing this! I was on oxygen for approximately three months. One day, he came home and said he was taking a motorcycle "guy trip" for the weekend to the casino in West Virginia. I was so mad I couldn't see straight. I didn't care if he took a "guy trip," I cared that he wouldn't spend the money to fix the house, so I could get better but he'd go on a trip to a casino and spend the money. He'd offered to put me up in a hotel if I wanted for thirty days! Then, I could come home and see if I was any better! I'd say, oh and then get sick all over again!

No thank you! I found a chemical on the Internet at Home Depot called Mold Control, and you could rent the machine to use it. It ended up costing $300 total. He finally went, got everything, and sprayed the entire house with it before he left. This was on a Friday, and by Saturday evening, I no longer needed the oxygen! When he returned home on Sunday, he asked me what had happened, why I wasn't on my oxygen. I told him the Mold Control worked!

We spent many hours planning long trips to places I'd never been. He was going to Australia to visit his son, and it was one place I'd always dreamed of going. I applied for and received my passport because he told me he was taking me with him. I happened to read a text message between him and his son. He'd told Spencer, "I'm telling the 'girlfriend' that you bought my ticket and not one for her so that she can't come!"

Spencer's reply was, "Daddy-O, I'm so proud of you. I didn't think you still had it in you!"

When I asked Scot, he simply said, "Spencer bought my ticket, and you can't go."

Eventually, I found out that all the planning for those trips were just make-believe and lies. He had no intention of taking me anywhere.

We went to New York to visit his daughter a couple of times, and in spite of the mean things he and his family said about her, I found her to be a very pleasant, confident, and a well-centered woman, considering the father she grew up with. Personally, I enjoyed each visit, even after she had her baby and was a little cranky! We, women, all go through that!

When Scot was in Australia, his mother and I had lunch one day. I had spoken my concerns to her of his lying all the time. Her only remark to me was, "If I'd known you had a problem with someone lying, I'd have told you to leave him a long time ago. He's not told the truth since he was five years old!" What can one say to that!

While Scot was in Australia, he only called me one time. He told me that he'd been too busy. I'd thought maybe he'd taken someone else with him because he'd gone so far as to tell me *not* to pick him up from the airport upon his return! When he returned from Australia, he did come home in a "taxi." When he came in the door, he threw his suitcase down and threw me over the couch with my face smashed in the couch and had his way with me. When he was done, he replied, "Whoa, I needed that," then got his suitcase and went upstairs.

The next day, I asked him about what his mom told me. His response was, "I don't lie! If I believe what I'm saying it's the truth, it's not a lie!"

My response was, "So, when you go to court, you're sworn under oath, you tell the judge you mailed these notices to the tenants when you didn't; what you are telling me is because you believe yourself, it's the truth?"

Scot responded, "Yes! Now you get it!"

I said, "I'm not going to court with you anymore. I will *not* lie or be a part of it."

I would come home from "managing his apartments, flipping and upgrading them," only to find towels hanging wet in our bathroom, as well as big wet spots on our bed. There were so many other things that were out of place such as food was eaten and left out. Doors left open or unlocked, just so much left in disarray. He'd tell me I was crazy and imagining all of it! Then I saw that he was tracking an ex-girlfriend and having lunch with her as well as being on several dating sites. He told me that the dating sites "wouldn't allow him to delete his profile!" I wasn't born yesterday; I knew he was lying and seeing others. I went so far as to pretend to be someone else and hit on him on a site. Needless to say, he fell for it.

Our relationship continued to get worse. We started seeing a marriage counselor, and Scot tried to convince him I was depressed, insane, and had a mental problem. I saw the counselor also on my own. He was taking steps to help me prepare to leave Scot. We both knew Scot would never change and had some serious mental issues. I was becoming terrified of him.

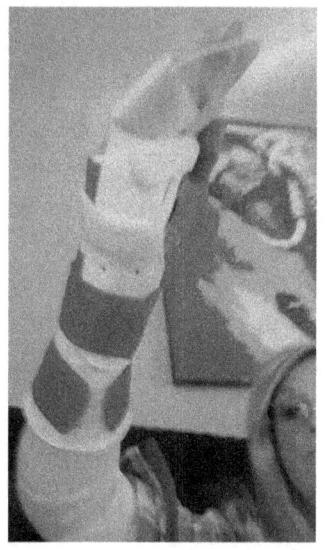

I'd had elbow surgery in January and was pretty much helpless for the next six weeks. I'd torn a tendon working at his apartments. He told me he was too busy to help me. I hired a housekeeper, and she helped to the point of even helping me shower. She despised him for his treatment of me.

The cast I had on my arm after surgery when Scot called the police and told them I fired my gun in the house. How could I have done this with this cast one?

I'd had enough. I tried to leave several times, but he would keep me in the bathroom by standing in the doorway and then throwing me back if I came near him, threatening to call the police. He'd already called them several times, and it was always my fault. I could never call because he'd take my phone away from me. I did have a weapon, one night, he fired it in an upper bedroom, and when I went up to the room, he called the police telling them I tried to shoot him. I told the police, "How could I possibly shoot my gun with my arm and hand in this full brace and cast?" Scot backtracked and said he wanted it put in his safe, so it couldn't happen again. The police asked me if I would agree to it. I said only under the conditions that I have the code, and be shown how to open the safe. All of us went out to the garage, and he was ordered to give me the code and teach me how to open it, as it was an old and complicated safe.

About a week later, Scot lost his keys and accused me of taking them. So, he began to tear the house apart, and started throwing stuff everywhere. I was very scared because I knew what would come next. I'd either be locked in a room or thrown outside with no coat or shoes and locked out of the house as he always does. Instead, I got my purse, my keys, went to the car, and started to get in, when all of a sudden, Scot was there, and he punched me in the face, broke a finger on my left hand, and sprained another finger. My left hand was all I could use, although I was now going to physical therapy for my right elbow and surgery. When he punched me in the face, right in my left eye, he broke my glasses. I'd never been punched by anyone in my life. Strangled, yes, but never hit or punched.

The first blackeye Scot gave me. I thought it was an accident.

He told me it was an accident; he didn't mean to do it. He just didn't want me to leave. He'd found his keys in the couch where he sat and must have lost them there. I went back inside with him, thinking to myself, yes, it must have been an accident. The next day, he took me with him on all of his errands and was sweet as honey to me. He kept telling me how much he loved me, and all we were going to do together. On the way back home, he looked at me and told me, "I feel so bad for what I did to you; you don't deserve to be treated like that."

I replied, "No, I don't, and if you ever do it again, *I will leave you.*"

He told me; looking at my face, he felt like he should take me home and lay me on a bed of rose petals. Yes, you're right, that should never have happened!

The next day, he had to go to his mom's to stay with her for the day to care for her because she'd been in the hospital sick. I went to my physical therapy. It did not go very well. My physical therapist was not too happy when she saw me. She asked me what happened, and I tried to lie. However, I ended up telling her the truth because I do not lie very well. She emailed my orthopedic doctor telling him what happened to me. He told her to have me come down and get x-rays, which I did. I had braces put on my fingers; they called security, and the social worker, who wanted me to press charges. I refused, telling them it was really an accident, and if it ever happened again, I would press charges and leave him. Reluctantly, they allowed me to go. I knew from him and what had already happened in our past, the local police would not do anything to him.

When I left, I went to his mom's as he'd asked me to do. I was standing in the kitchen when I heard, Scot, one of his sisters, and their mom who were in her bedroom. No one knew I was there yet. I hear Scot telling them how clumsy I am and how I'd fallen, and my face had hit the wall giving me a black eye and hurting my fingers. They were all laughing at me. Then his sister said to Scot, "Well, is the little "f-b-" going to let you stay and help our mom today?""

He replied, "He does whatever he wants, and doesn't care about me." (At this time of our relationship, I'd started recording him and our conversations and fights because I was terrified of him and his lies.)

Just then, she walked into the kitchen and saw me standing there. I asked if she really wanted to know what happened to me and proceeded to tell her. She called me a liar and said, "Now I really hate you," and left.

Scot came out asking what I was doing there. I said, "really, you told me to come here after my appointment!"

Of course, he denied it. We fought, and I left.

When I went to counseling the next day, I told him what happened. There were various times I'd called him when I was stranded outside in zero degree weather or when I was terrified of Scot. The counselor asked me if I really wanted to be in a relationship with Scot. The counselor told me, that Scot was not worth it and what could I possibly see in him. At that point, I told the counselor I'm terrified of what he'll do to me if I try to leave again. I also told him that I had a very bad gut feeling about his "upcoming family vacation." I just didn't want to go. I knew something really bad was going to happen. I had told Scot I didn't want to go so, he bought my son a ticket, ensuring me going.

His family was planning a big Disney World vacation in Florida in March. As I said, I just didn't want to go.

A week before we left on vacation, he had me copy all of my documents: driver's license, social security card, bank cards (both of ours), birth certificate, and any other type of document that I had. He then had me email the copies to *him* and myself on his office computers. He said it is always best to do this when you travel just in case you lose something. My wallet had already been stolen on one trip with him to New York to visit his daughter. So, I thought he knew what he was talking about even though we'd never done this before. God was talking to me and very loud.

Scot wrote in a journal every morning. This is what he wrote eight weeks exactly before he beat me up.

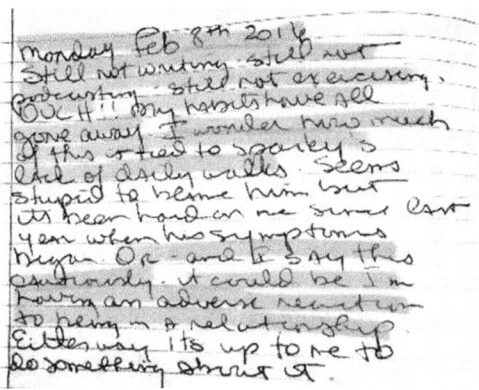

(Scot wrote in a journal every morning. This is what he wrote eight weeks exactly before he beat me up.) When I found this I felt as if he had something planned, he was blaming me.

The "him" he is referring to is his dog that was at death's door when I met him, nursed back to life, and assumed his responsibility. When I look back now, I can almost see him preparing for what happened while on vacation. I had a very sick feeling in the pit of my stomach. When I'd go to my counseling session, I would tell him of my deep concerns. The next day, the doctor would have me voice my concerns in our session. It was as if Scot was trying to make me appear to be psychotic or very depressed when it was he who was manipulating both the doctor and me.

Where Is God in My Path of Faith?

Where is God in my life here! He, the Holy Spirit. and the Angels were surrounding me protecting me. They were telling me, warning me to get away from this man, and "not to take this trip." I didn't listen this time, but they were right there with me. Tell me, can you see this?

Scripture

> For He guards the course of the just and protects the way of his faithful ones. (Proverbs 2:8, NLT)

Praise

Father, please protect me as I go forth from here. Please send your Angels to protect and guard my children and me. Amen.

Chapter 19

My First Glimpse of Domestic Violence

This is how the hardest time of my life began. As always, I have to own up to my part in it and forgive the others for myself, not them.

For yet another time, I sought out love, and it was the wrong place. This time, I paid a very high price and learned a very big lesson of how to survive domestic abuse. I did not know any of the signs of domestic abuse, so I couldn't have recognized them. Now, I see it from the moment he first talked to me.

I do have to say; this is the hardest part of my book to write. I've been putting it off because I do not want to relive it.

Scot had told me leading up to the family vacation how he couldn't wait to show me and take me around Disney World for the first time. He said it would be like the first time for him seeing it through my eyes and my son's. Having asked him several times, what about Bridgette, his youngest daughter (twenty-eight or so) and her two young daughters? He spent a lot of time with his granddaughters since Bridgette had them a couple of times a week. She'd have him watch the girls because "she needed her time, and it was just too much work on her to work part-time, to be able to 'party' and take care of the girls a couple of days." This was said to him and me several times a week. Then, Scot and Bridgette would have to have their "Daddy-Daughter time." What it was, I never knew because I was not allowed to be involved. All I know is that when Bridgette called Daddy, he ran to her, not any of his other children, just her. He told me we'd only spend one day with them because he wanted to be with Michael and me.

Scot, Michael, Scot's sister, two children, and I were driving there in Bridgette's SUV, so she would have a car down there. We planned on a two day/night trip with all of us taking turns driving. Upon arrival, Scot got a rental car because when Bridgette flew in with the girls, she took over the SUV, and no one could touch it, especially me. Our first day came when we could go to the park. We spent the day with Bridgette and the girls doing whatever they wanted. The second day, it was the same. Michael was only going to be there for four days and flying back on the fifth for school. I wanted him to enjoy adult activities while there. Bridgette threw her temper tantrum, like always, and I ended up being the bad person, even in my son's eyes. He told me, "It's okay, Mom, I don't mind being with the girls." I asked Scot one night what happened to him wanting to show Michael and me around the park and his promise "to not always being" with Bridgette.

He would wake up in the morning, not even tell me good morning, but run over to her cabin to tell her good morning! He started getting meaner toward me when we were alone, which was not a lot. Just like at home, he did this while no one was around to witness. He'd stay in his mother's cabin drinking and getting high with her or go to Bridgette's or one of his sisters' cabins. Michael and I began going to the park to get on adult rides by ourselves. Scot, when I started working on his apartment buildings, had given me a credit card and a bank card, but never paid me, we each also had a certain amount of money for food and drinks on our Disney bands.

Honestly, I felt very bad for Michael, but he too was mad at me, taking Scot's side. No matter what I did, I was always wrong in everyone's eyes. Scot made sure no one knew the real truth of what was going on. Scot was always the happy, clown, fun person everyone wanted to be around. But, when we were alone or at home, it was as if he was exhausted from being that nice person. He actually reminded me of how Mom had been. Scot's family had a window business, which his mom and dad started years ago, and each kid had a trust fund. Scot was kicked out of the business, for what, I have no idea of the real truth, only his lies. It didn't really matter to me. He was the kind of person that took from everyone else, including his own children, and never paid it back until he was tied down and threatened. The utilities were always being shut off, especially at the apartments, and he wanted me to lie to the companies to cover for him. His mom gave him a loan to cover a debt at the apartments for taxes. Anyway, what I'm trying to say is he takes and uses any and everyone while making you feel like it's you, your fault, or maybe you're going crazy, and everyone believes him and won't even listen to you.

Back to the vacation, as you can tell, it was going bad. March 28 came, and it was time for Michael to fly home. Scot and I were taking him to the Sanford Airport in Florida. Scot orders me to the back seat, as if I'm not the adult but his little toy. Due to my asthma, breathing problems, and being barricaded in rooms by him, I've become claustrophobic.

On the way to the airport, I had an asthma attack; Scot had my inhaler, wouldn't give it to me, open a window, or even stop for me. I called 911 telling them he's pretty much kidnapped me, and relay all of this to them. Now, he stops to wait for the police. Scot and Michael are both unhappy with me and yelling at me. What's new, right! Michael is calling me some pretty bad names, and as much as I hate this, I admit it, I did it, I slapped him. He then tells me he hates me. What else is new, right? Scot just smiled. When the police arrive, they talk separately to Scot and me. Scot had some marijuana on him and told them it was mine for medicinal purposes! When asked if it was mine I replied, "No, could I please get my inhaler?"

The police gave it to me. Scot, of course, lies his way out of everything and puts the blame on everyone else, and we're free to go. I know this is a bit off track, but I have to say this. Scot would throw anyone "under the bus."

I witnessed many times him doing the same with his own daughters. He would be with his family, and his sisters and mom would be making fun of them or putting them down. Scot would join right in. If I were there, I would always stand up for both of the girls. I never said a bad word about them. They both gave their Dad loans that they had to beg him to pay back, and he would actually complain to me about. He would tell me how they were both cranky or he'd call them more "colorful words," especially Bridgette. Being a parent myself, it made me sick to my stomach, and we fought a lot over this, but when we would be with them, he'd tell them I said these things about them!

Back to the airport, meanwhile, Scot takes my phone from me and sends me again to the back seat. Michael was not talking to me; he'd said how he felt. He and Scot talked and laughed about what happened as if I'm not even there. Something I'm quite used to in my life. I don't exist to anyone.

We dropped Michael off at the airport. He allowed me to hug him, but I had a feeling I wouldn't be seeing him again just like his sister and brother. I've completely failed, as a mother, daughter, sister, wife, everything. I was very upset and not feeling very well.

I got in the front seat of the car, and Scot started to drive around to the exit. At this time, I said, "Scot, could I please have my phone back?"

Scot replied, "No fckng, B."

I said, "Scot, it's my phone, I pay for it, give it to me, please."

I then reached with my right hand over to him to get my phone sitting between his legs. Before I knew what was going on, he began pounding on my face several times and my right arm and leg, but he was continuing to drive until we got to a grassy area. He then stops and drags me out by my hair and starts slamming my head on the car, while continuing to hit me more. I knew he was going to kill me. A truck is driving by, but it stops. I hear a man yell, "Do you need help?" I see there's a man and woman in the truck, so I yelled the best I can, "Yes, he's going to kill me."

With that, Scot grabbed my hair, and as he was saying, "The best thing you can do right now is get in this car, and we'll drive out of here like nothing ever happened."

With that, he threw me in the car and proceeded to drive to the exit where the police stopped him, and arrested him. They kept me for a long time taking my statement, pictures, and the statement of the witnesses. The police asked me why he had some blood on his face! I said to them, "Look at me, I'm completely covered in blood from him beating me, he doesn't even have a scratch."

They all agreed. When I went to leave, I was told I had to take a taxi because they allowed him to have the rental car returned. On my taxi ride back, I also discovered that he'd been allowed to cancel all of my bank and credit cards before they took him away. (God again!) I had the exact money for the taxi fare. Upon arrival at the cabins where everyone was staying, his entire family descended upon me. One sister and his mother said to me, "What did you do to make him do this?"

Another sister said, "Look at her, she didn't make him."

His mom was yelling at me that I had to leave she didn't want me there. I simply said, "With what? I have nothing."

Then they were all arguing and yelling at me, so I went into our cabin and locked the door.

A few minutes later, the police were knocking at the door. I had to let them in, and the female officer said they'd received a call saying I had drugs, a gun, and that I was going to kill myself. The male officer just started ripping through everything looking for the so-called items that I had. I looked at the female officer crying and said, "Look at me; Do I look like I'm going to hurt myself anymore then he's hurt me? He almost killed me. The drugs are his, and my gun is in his safe at home."

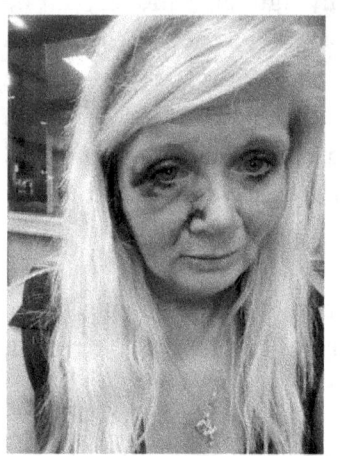

This is how I looked right after Scot beat me up at the airport in Florida.

She looked me over and replied, "Yup, he put a real hurtin' on you. That's gonna be real bad in the mornin'."

They went back outside to the family to talk. A few minutes later, both came back in, and I was told I had to leave. I explained what he'd done with the money, the cards, and that I had nothing. Both again went back outside for a little while. When they came back in, I was told Disney would put me up for two nights, two days at another resort at no charge, and on the third day, I'd have to leave. I said, "And then what do I do, how do I get home?"

The male police officer said, "Look, do you really want to stay here with these kinds of people? They all seem to be drunk and high on something? Let's get you packed up and moved out of here."

I really had no choice. Another taxi delivered me to a Disney Resort. Where it was or what it was called, I honestly have no idea. I literally went into the room terrified of how I was going to get home, so I called my older son who lives in Florida. He told me, "I don't have time for this right now. I can't help you."

He was literally only four hours from where I was. He's not had me be a part of his life since then. His girlfriend told me, it's his choice, and he doesn't want me in their lives. However, they are born-again Christians living the life of Christ! Next, I did the only other thing I could think of, but with very little hope because I had no one in my life. Scot made sure of that. I went to Facebook, and to my surprise, on his page, he had a picture of him and his entire family bragging about the wonderful Kenkel Disney Family Vacation. I was on fire, mad, hurt and in shock still. I posted on his page a picture and description of what he'd done to me. Then, I went to my Facebook page and posted photos of what he'd done to me with a description and pleading for help to get home. I had very little hope in anything at this time. I was more scared at this time then when I lived in my car for eight months. I couldn't think anymore, and I passed out for that night and the next day.

The following are pictures I've taken at the hotel and on my four day Greyhound bus ride home, which the domestic violence advocate told me to continue taking. I had not even seen what he had done to me yet, besides my torn clothes.

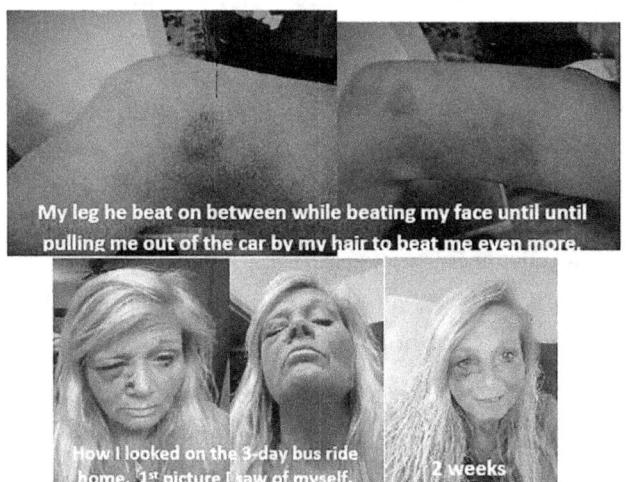

These are the pictures I had to take following Scot beating me. I had to take them up to two week afterwards for the Florida Attorney General's Office to prosecute him. I looked like this too on the four-day bus ride back home.

These are only a few of the pictures. I had fingerprints up and down my thighs, legs, and my arms. There were very distinctive fingerprints, on my arms, legs along with very big, bad bruises a lot of places including a black eye, chin, and nose. I didn't even think of looking at myself, I just hurt so much and was, well honestly, in severe shock.

I was very shocked when I saw myself, having never been hit even once in my life other than that first time I thought he'd "accidently given a black eye. No one ever deserves to be abused like this. Mental and emotional abuse is bad and lasts a lifetime, but this puts the fear of everything into you.

Where Is God in My Path of Faith?

Where isn't God in my life here! I Say again, He, the Holy Spirit and the Angels were surrounding and protecting me. They'd warned me, to get away from this man and "not to take this trip." Even though I went, they were with there loving me and taking care of me, placing so many people in my life to help me along the way. Did you see them? Do you see them in your life too?

Scripture

> He is the God who pays back those who harm me; he brings down the nations under me. (2 Samuel 22:48, NLT)
> You are my refuge and my shield; your word is my source of hope. (Psalm 119:114, NLT)

Praise

Heavenly Father, thank you for never leaving me; you were always defending, protecting, and carrying me when I could no longer walk.

Chapter 20

God Sends His Angels to Me

The next evening when I awakened, I received a phone call from a friend I knew from back in 2010 who had lived in Kentucky. Do you remember me talking about Jim? I went to AA meetings with him and cooked him dinners? He had a girlfriend that was an addict, and he just disappeared. He is the friend who called me and helped me. Sounds like a wonderful guy, right! I thought so too! At least he's reaching out and helping me now. Thank you, Jesus. He saw on my Facebook what had happened to me and told me he was buying me a bus ticket home and arranging a ride to the bus terminal the next day. I was very relieved but still in a state of shock. I fell back asleep, and the next morning, I left for the bus terminal.

The ride home took over the next four days. I'd had nothing to eat or drink for days now. I was exhausted, in a state of shock, looked horrible, and I was lost. We went to some very undesirable terminals for layovers, which scared me even more. I was scared of my own shadow by this time. On one of my layovers, a young girl, about twenty-six, came up to me and said; "I'm sorry for what you're going through. Please, go get some food and something to drink," and she placed some money in my hand. (God again!) "For I was hungry, and you gave me something to eat, I was thirsty, and you gave me something to drink, I was a stranger, and you invited me in" (Matthew 25:35–40, NLT).

I'd not said anything to anyone! Yes, Christ and the angels are here with me even if I can't see it at this time.

Scot's sister kept calling me on my bus ride home. She was passing his threat on, saying that Scot and the police were going to press charges against me for calling the police on the way to the airport earlier if I didn't drop the charges on him. They just didn't understand, the State of Florida is prosecuting. Why does anyone not understand, it is now out of my hands. I will now only be a witness. Then, I received a call from Scot's friend, Michael, saying he was at the house waiting for me. I told him there is a restraining order against Scot, his family, and friends. He was not to be at that house when I returned home. He said, well, I'm just here to help you! I told him, no you have to leave. Calling my Domestic Violence Advocate scared to death of what was going to happen; I was advised to call the "local police!" When I called the local police, I was told to come to the police station first, and they'd escort me to the house. When I arrived, I was told to wait; the officers were at the house with Scot's friend and sister!

When they returned to the station, they told me that they knew nothing about a restraining order or of Scot doing anything wrong! I showed them the papers I had from Florida, but they were not good enough. The officers said they'd need direct proof from Florida. The Florida State Attorney's Office even faxed them the "official papers," but I was told, again, not good enough! I was never escorted home. When I reached home, the car I drove was gone, as well as my belongings inside it. Going inside and looking around, I saw that the officers had allowed Scot's sister and friend to go through the house in the time I was detained at the station and take whatever they'd been instructed by Scot to take, including my belongings.

Scot had everything, but the water and electric turned off in the house. Jim, who was the one that bought my bus ticket back home, came to visit with his dad. Jim wanted me to come live at his dad's house in Lima, Ohio, to help with his dad's care until I could get on my feet. I was talking to my friend, Cheryl, in Chicago and contemplating going there for a couple of weeks, but then what? Jim and his dad spent the night encouraging me while I packed. While spending the night, Jim is trying to talk me into being his girlfriend. I keep asking him about his girlfriend back home. He just says that she's in jail, and they've broken up. I explain to him, I in no way want a relationship with anyone in that way. I cannot handle anything like that. I only need to work on myself and my relationship with God. I know I'm a mess and do not ever want another relationship with anyone else but God. I am here to serve Him until my dying day. I explain this to both Jim and Harry (Jim's dad). They both say they completely understand, and we agreed I'd come to stay while I recuperate, but only to help with Harry's caretaking. The next day, they leave taking some of my most valuable possessions with them and some I didn't know Jim took.

I said I would go back to Florida to testify the following Monday because I was told it would help the prosecution against Scot if I were to appear in Sanford, Florida. I had no money to get there. However, a gofundme.com account was set up on Facebook, and there were a few generous donations, which helped me to fly back and forth and then to move.

I was to fly to Sanford, Florida, on Sunday to prepare for court on Monday. This is not something I want to do, but I said I would go because I was asked by the State of Florida Attorney General's Office to appear and testify. As you've gathered by now, I always do what is asked of me and what is right, no matter the consequences to me. Sunday morning, I boarded a plane to Florida once again. I was greeted with a police escort to a shelter where I spent the night so I could go to court and back to the airport. The Sanford, Florida, Police were wonderful as they stayed with me until I was safely on-boarded on the plane heading home! When I was at the shelter, employees, counselors, and the women staying there talked to me. I learned more about domestic violence than I ever wanted to know, but the women were all wonderful, and I still pray for them every day.

My Domestic Violence Advocate picked me up for court Monday morning. I was interviewed by the state attorney and others. Florida's Attorney General's office, State Attorney's office, and the Domestic Violence Office are some of the most wonderful and helpful people that I came across in this desperate time. What I've learned from this is that if any one state needs to learn how to treat its victims, they need to take lessons from the State of Florida, at least in Sanford, Florida. We all went to a conference room to wait. I was shaking with fear of having to see him again. They were trying to calm me and work it out so I'd not have to see Scot.

A plea bargain was going on, but Scot refused to admit what he'd done to me. As usual, it was me and he'd done nothing wrong. At one point, his attorney asked permission to see me. I agreed he could. He walked in, looked at me, and walked out. A plea was then reached more quickly. Scot was to have an ankle-tracking bracelet for nine months, was not allowed to enter the house until May 1, 2016, when I was to vacate it. We had a permanent injunction against him (restraining order), and he was to pay me for three months' rent at $750 per month. He also had to attend a drug and alcohol treatment program as well as a domestic violence/anger management program. He was to attend both of these programs in Sanford, Florida.

He was also to be randomly tested for drug use. The case would be reviewed randomly by the judge in Court. After a year, the judge would make a final decision. I fought to make sure that the programs were not on the Internet because Scot was a "licensed real estate broker and agent." He was only this on paper because when testing/renewal time came, he would pay his friend. Michael Leta (the friend waiting for me at the home), to go and take the testing for him because, of course, he was just too busy to take it himself. Scot claimed that no one ever knew the difference. I also knew he would do the same if these programs were online. I was told he had to report to Florida for the programs. (God again!)

MY PATH OF FAITH

Where Is God in My Path of Faith?

I would never say "God allowed" any of this to happen. But, I do see him place his angels everywhere in my path to help me get through. The devil kept trying to attack and break me down. He had his Holy Protectors and all of Heaven protecting me even if I was unaware at the time. "Here is where I see God in my Path of Faith: someone stopping to help me, and it caused him to be arrested; Disney putting me up in another resort; a person giving me a bus ticket and ride; a girl giving me money for food and drink; the Domestic Violence Team; and the gofundme.com donations; my protectors when I returned to face him again, and the protection of never having to see or face him again."

Scripture

> For He will order his **angels to protect you** wherever you go. (Psalm 91:11, NLT)

Praise

Thank you for seeking me, Lord, even when I was lost and in need.

Chapter 21

Completely Broken by Domestic Violence

Upon my return, I sat in this big, lonely house with my cat, Sam. Scot was to make arrangements through the "local police department," at my convenience, to "pick up a few of his items." I knew how Scot was and how his family was with the local police department. That had already been shown to me. I was living in fear every day, of his family and friends. They would periodically drive by the house, call me, and threaten me. I left one time to go to the doctors, and upon my return, the locks were changed, and items were missing. Calling the police department, I was told it was a domestic problem, and they wouldn't respond. I tried to explain to them it wasn't, I had the papers and the Attorney General's office had already faxed the papers to them. It did me no good. They would not listen to me. I had to break the back door, and then I changed the locks myself.

The only thing I could do was begin packing what little I had left. I had no money (the money I had was to be used for moving), no food, only water. Luckily, Sam still had some food. I sat there by myself with my cat, Sam, for a week. I have to say; I was terrified and over thinking everything. Starting to think, or rather, getting that gut feeling that going to Lima, Ohio, to live with Jim and his dad wasn't such a good idea. That something bad was going to happen there.

He kept calling me every day to see how I was and when I'd be there. Never once did he offer to help with my move. All I wanted was to feel my Father's love and peace and just to stop all of the turmoil and fear. My fear, the shock of what had happened, and what will happen, never could I go back with Scot, and I never wanted to see him. His family, their threats, not feeling safe where I was; and, my own children were not speaking to me now.

I was feeling totally alone it was so overwhelming that I forgot I had a God bigger than anything and that He would pull me through anything. Instead, all I wanted was to stop hurting from the life that I've lived and the fear that I was in. All I wanted was to feel my Father wrap himself around me with his loving light of grace, forgiveness, and unconditional love and hold me.

I hate to admit this, but at my weakest moment of being beaten down and in shock, I broke. Instead of crying out for Jesus as I always did, I drank some antifreeze, so I could go home. I didn't think of it as taking my life or dying; I was getting rid of all of the pain, the fear, the fighting, hurting, loneliness, and no love in my life. I just wanted to go home. I pray now that no one ever has to reach this point. I make a promise to everyone; I'll always be there for you if you need me. God does love each of us and wants us to live a wonderful life, even when you struggle. We are always here for you. Just reach out.

I wrote the following poem a long time ago because I know what this is like and never wanted anyone else to feel this.

BARBIE SCHUCHART-CARLISLE

A Lonely Day

To grow with the years and to be alone,
What a sadness that would be:

To only dream of yesterday and not of any tomorrows,
To wake each day with;
No plans, just hopes of what the day could bring.
To lay around and wait,
And wait, but for what?

To call someone but they're too busy,
To need a friend just... someone,
To help you pass away
A Lonely Day -
To help you see it through.

Do you ever wonder,
Just how they make it?
Never invited to laugh and dance?
To pass away a day with nothing else but time;
To be forgotten, lonely and blue;
With not a thing in the world for you alone to do...

How sad it is to have -
No plans of something, just anything to do.
You'd never know just how they feel
Until that day....
It happens to you.

Barbie (Buck) Schuchart
Published and Awarded By the International Poet Society
International Poet of the Year (July 2008)

MY PATH OF FAITH

Before I did the unthinkable, I printed out all of the pictures I'd been taking of myself of where I was beat up which I'd been taking for the Attorney General's Office and stapled them to the walls everywhere in the house. I wanted Scot to see what he'd done to me.

My youngest son, Michael's, birthday is April 7, and I had texted him asking if he would come over. He'd replied, I don't know, maybe on Friday, which was April 8. He was still very angry with me, which is understandable. I honestly, never wanted my children to live through any of what I'd put them through. Again, I slept and just lay on the couch peeking out my window to see if anyone was going to break in. Wednesday, the eighteenth, is when I broke. Michael had not come over nor had he even called or text me. I really hadn't expected him to. Not really thinking about what I was doing, only about how I was feeling, I poured myself some pop with some antifreeze and drank it. I think I remember walking upstairs and then trying to come back down.

When I got downstairs, I think I just fell on the floor; I'm not too sure. I was crying and said, please help me, Father, I can't do this anymore. I'm told Michael found me on Friday and called 911. I was dead but taken to the hospital. No one knew what I had done as there was no evidence. After I'd poured the antifreeze, I made sure I replaced the bottle where it belonged before drinking it. Eventually, they found my cretin level was at 27 (normal is .05–1). I was put on dialysis. I don't know what else. All I can remember was seeing these beautiful streaks of different colors of light all around me and thinking, I must be in a special place in heaven and the angels are taking care of me. I don't know how long I was like this, but when I finally was revived, the kidney doctor came in and told me that I was not going to live because no one ever lives after this. If I did live, I'd be on dialysis all my life.

The psychiatrist came in and started yelling at me. All I can remember is thinking I didn't try to kill myself, I just want to go home. I thought he was the devil, and he scared me. I fell in and out of consciousness for a while. The kidney doctor kept coming back and telling me I wasn't going to live. About a week later, my cretin level had gone down to 13, and she was still holding on to "you're not going to live, or you'll be on dialysis all your life." I couldn't remember anyone's phone number, and my son didn't want to talk to me. It didn't really matter because I couldn't even talk, move my fingers, or remember my own name for a while. Eventually, I remembered one friend's number, and he actually did come to talk to me. I look at the picture of what I looked like after two weeks, and I did look like death.

A couple of days later the doctor came in again with her same words, but my cretin had gone down to 9 now. This time, she said, "Well I don't know if you'll live, but if you do, you will be on dialysis all your life." That night, I said a prayer to God. It wasn't if you do this I'll do that. It was a prayer of total surrender to His will of what He wanted for me. Simply saying. "God, if You want me to die, I accept that; if You want me to live and be on dialysis, I accept that; if You want me to live as a healthy person, I accept that. Whatever You want of me, I accept. I am here only for You and will live only for You and do Your work and Your Will forever. God, You know my heart, and I wasn't trying to die but to stop all the hurting. So, whatever You want, I am Yours. I pray this in Jesus Name, Amen."

What I looked like in the hospital on dialysis after coming to from drinking antifreeze, being found and pronounced DOA 2 days later. This picture was a week and a half later.

The next morning, they drew my blood, and a few hours later, the doctor came in, stating not her usual but, "I'm not sure what happened, but your cretin level is at 2.7. You can move to the step-down level and go home in a couple of days, but we'll do dialysis three days a week to see what it's going to do."

I smiled and said, "I know what happened, I have more work to do!"

> God the Father knew you and chose you long ago and his Spirit has made you holy. As a result, you have obeyed him and have been cleansed by the blood of Jesus Christ. May God give you more and more grace and peace. (1 Peter 1:2, NLT)

I was moved to a step-down level continuing the dialysis. Scot was due to appear in court again, so I started getting visitors at the hospital. First, his friend, Michael, came to see me. He was on his way to Florida and wanted me to fly there and tell the court that Scot didn't do anything to me. I told him, no. He did do it. Next, Scot's sister, Angie (who'd been calling and threatening me), appeared in my room. Within seconds, nurses and aids were in my room ready to remove her. I told them I'd hear what she has to say. With that, she pretty much told me that because of what I did I was crazy and needed to be locked away and that her brother did not do anything to me. I then asked her to leave. She said she'd be back. What she didn't know was that the hospital security would be waiting for her on her next visit.

The next day, I was discharged from the hospital, returning home via Uber! I was to do three more dialysis treatments and see what my cretin level was. I took an Uber each time, and at the end of my treatments, my cretin was down to 1.7. The doctor said I no longer needed dialysis! There was one week left in the month, and I had to be out by May 1. I did lay around still depressed and in shock, wondering how was I going to load the U-Haul truck (which Jim's brother, Garth, had graciously gotten me a discount because he works there) by myself and move? Again, God placed an angel in my life!

An old school friend who said he and his son would come over Saturday, April 30, and load the truck for me! An old tenant and his wife and friend were also supposed to come and help. They'd come to the hospital and actually sold me a car they had for my last $750! They never showed up, and I never received the car either! Joey and Nicole disappeared stealing my money! I'd given them a break moving them into the apartments as they'd been homeless! Great payback! That's on them, not me!

Now it's May 1, 2016. I'm moving to Lima, Ohio, against everything I was feeling. My friend and his son did come, load the truck, then Sam and I were on our way to Lima. Somewhere I'd never been before, and it was four hours away. I felt like maybe I'd be a little safer when we got there.

Where Is God in My Path of Faith?

If God brings you back to life, cleans you up inside, he thinks you are worth saving. I believe deeply he has a purpose for me, which I need to fulfill. This isn't the first time He's done, this, right!

Scripture

> For it is by grace you have been saved, through faith—and this is not from yourselves, it is the gift of God—not by works, so that no one can boast. (Ephesians 2:8–9, NLT)

Praise

Heavenly Father, thank you for cleaning me up inside, for thinking I was worth saving and for giving me another chance to do your work.

Chapter 22

He Thought I Was Worth Saving, so He Cleaned Me Up Inside

Sam and I arrived in Lima, Ohio, late Saturday afternoon. Jim, his dad, and some of his friends that came to help unload the U-Haul greeted me. Jim and I had been calling throughout my four hour trip from Kentucky to Lima, Ohio. Jim's friends unloaded the truck, storing all my belongings in a side room, instructed by Harry, Jim's dad. Jim asked if I wanted to share his bedroom with him, but I declined, telling him again, "I'm not ready for any type of relationship, we are friends, I appreciate what you and Harry are doing, but I need to work on myself and find myself again."

So Jim's friends set me up in a back bedroom. Jim was not very happy with me. He left, and Harry told me that Jim thought we were going to be a couple, but he'd been telling him just what I'd said, "She's in no place to be in a relationship, and she told you that."

Besides helping with Harry, I hid in my room with Sam or sat on the couch talking to Harry. I contacted the Domestic Violence Shelter and was set up for counseling. Harry took me to get a new birth certificate, social security card, and helped me to buy clothing that had been stolen from me by Scot's family and friends while I was in the hospital. They'd actually taken one of each of my shoes/boots, all of my jeans, most of my shorts, my panties, and bras. Jim was the one that was supposed to be helping me, but he stayed away all the time, and Harry was not happy with him. However, Harry and I began to get to know each other, became friends, and I actually started trusting someone. Harry finally told me that Jim had gotten back with his girlfriend before I came there to live. In fact, they'd never broken up, she'd just been in jail for driving on a suspended license, and she was very angry with me for coming there to live.

She had the impression Jim and I were "living together." Jim would bring her over, and she'd stay in the car. One night, I went out to meet her, and she cursed me up one side and down the other. I asked her if she knew why I was there. She stated, to be with Jim. I tried to tell her the truth and show her pictures, but she was too busy screaming at me. I just walked away because I cannot handle screaming or fighting, especially now.

Having no car to get around, I started looking and found one in Cleveland, Ohio. My naïve side thought the two brothers of the dealership were doing me a favor as they said they were! Jim and Harry drove me there one day to buy the car. Jim came in with me, and as I was filling out all the paperwork, he told the owner about how he served prison time for being a trafficker and dealer of drugs. He told him all about his drug life. I was so embarrassed and could tell the owner was too. The car was purchased with the money from Scot who had paid me one time, the $750, and never again. With that money and the rest of my saved money, I was able to purchase the car. Finally, I was on my way to being independent again! It didn't matter if it wasn't the best car in the world, it was mine!

The Florida Attorney General's office, along with the Domestic Violence Department was going to pay me $1,500.00 for relocation. I'd submitted all of my receipts with the help of a counselor and waited. Lima's DV Department and Ohio Attorney General's office didn't like the idea and they were very reluctant. Florida's AG had to call Ohio's AG and the DV Shelter Director and confirm it was what they do but they have to send it to the shelter. I was, however, attending Domestic Violence (DV) awareness classes, which the shelter held every Thursday evening. Also, I'd been going weekly to a psychiatrist, via Skype, at the local clinic and talking to two other of their counselors.

In the beginning, the psychiatrist was so worried about me that he had me coming in three days a week. The medications he started me on made me feel numb and like I was drunk. I'd only taken two doses then tried to drive out the driveway and almost ran into the mailbox. Turning around and going home, I called the doctor's office and said I could not take these and was given an appointment the next day and switched medications. The psychiatrist had diagnosed me with PTSD, and the depression was only from shock from what Scot had done to me. He wrote a letter saying that my cat, Sam, was a medical support cat. All of the counselors and the psychiatrist were wonderful and very helpful. The support group I went to on Thursday evenings taught me so much about domestic violence. Things that I had no idea of and opened my eyes to see the truth of my part in believing Scot from the beginning and letting him use my shame to beat me down.

Harry told me to apply for a job at a drive through up the road. Mustering all I could, I went up and talked to Kathy. She was a happy, loud, boisterous person who would give anyone whatever he or she needed. She has the biggest heart of any person I've seen. She told me what time to come in the next day, and she'd start training me. For the next two weeks, I went through training in the store, at the drive-thru window, running errands, and anything else Kathy could think of to help me keep the job. Kathy and I had become friends. She too had gone through something similar to what I had gone through, so she understood.

The home situation was getting very bad. Jim was stealing and selling my property; he was bringing his girlfriend around, and there was so much screaming, yelling, and fighting between them. I was being threatened and there were drugs and drinking going on in the house. My PTSD was in high gear. My psychiatrist was telling me I needed to live somewhere else! Right, how and with what? I personally knew I could not do this job. I couldn't remember the long grocery lists people would tell me to get at the drive-thru window or the types of cigarettes. I knew nothing about cigarettes as I'd never smoked! At the end of the two weeks, Kathy and I talked and came to an agreement, I just couldn't work there. I felt like another failure but knew I couldn't. Kathy told me when it had happened to her it took her awhile to be able to remember things and to live a normal life. She also said, she knew the people where I was staying, and I needed to leave, if she didn't already have a tenant, she'd let me come with her.

While working at the store, my right thumb locked up and I was no longer able to use it. This began a long procession of orthopedic visits and physical therapy. One of the physical therapists told me, "It's just in your head because of what happened to you." I knew she was wrong. Something bad was wrong with my thumb as a result of what Scot had done to me. In the pictures, you could actually see his handprints on my wrist and up my arm. This information was all forwarded to the State Attorney's office at their request. These are the pictures that were sent, and the doctor used.

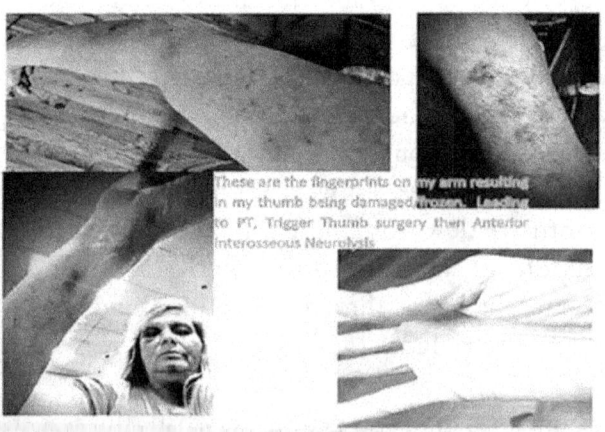

The bruises on my right arm and thumb which caused me to have Anterior Interosseous Neurolysis leading to two surgeries.

It was thrown up in my face every day by Jim what a failure I was that I'd lost my job. He then got me a job working where he worked. Driving for Steven Griffiths and his company, Easy Transit LLC. He worked for CareSource or one of the insurance companies, and he would have us drive patients to and from their doctor/hospital appointments. I probably drove a couple of thousand miles myself in one month's time. He was to pay for gas, as well as $10 an hour. My gas was never paid, and I was only paid for one week of work. My brakes on my car went out while driving a patient to the hospital, but luckily, we were right by the hospital. When I called Steve, he told me to keep driving! I refused, telling him it was too dangerous; he needed to call Jim and have him do it.

When he, Steve, finally reached Jim, he said he was too tired and that he'd been driving all day and wasn't finished yet. I dropped my car off at a friend's body shop, and they drove me home. Jim was there sleeping. What I found out was that Jim only drove his girlfriend to the suboxone clinic in Dayton, Ohio, every day then they go to the casino for the rest of the day and spend Harry's money. Sometimes, Harry even went with them. Whether Jim actually took her or not, he would still account for the time and mileage, turn it in, get reimbursed for the gas, and paid for the day. He said Steve knew and they both profited from it. When I asked Steve, he said well, I'm meeting with him tomorrow, but he does drive that. After that, I was never paid for my remaining weeks, and my living situation escalated. Jim's girlfriend had confronted me and realized that I'd not just appeared there as Jim had told her. Jim had said to her; "She was driving to Chicago one day and just dropped in and said, 'I'm going to live here.'" I never knew whether to trust her, if she was telling me the truth or lying. She was always high or drunk, and you could hear her talking bad about me all the time.

One of my counselors was trying to help me find work and a better place to live. One day, she suggested I try going to her church. No, I've not been to a church since the one in Kentucky where the pastor lied about me then had me fired. She kept insisting and said she'd be there. Reluctantly, I agreed to meet her that Sunday.

That Sunday, Jim and his girlfriend had gone to a casino, and Garth was there visiting. He had a warrant out for his arrest and didn't drive around Lima. He asked me to take him to get cigarettes, which I agreed. After he bought his cigarettes, he asked me to take him to his friend's house. This was going to make me late for church, and I despise being late for anything. If I'm on time, I'm late! But, I took him, and when I returned to the church, even though I was a few minutes late, people were still going in.

As I mentioned in my introduction:

> One of my counselors recommended a church to me about a month after I moved to where I'm now living. Since I moved here from Kentucky, I felt myself being pulled to the very same church every time I drove past. However, due to the bad experience I had with the pastor at the church I worked with in Kentucky for eight years, I hadn't been able to go back to any church. My PTSD had left me scared of doing many things. However, I went on Sunday, June 16, 2016!
>
> The minute I walked thru the doors, I looked to the back of the Sanctuary, I took in a deep breath, exhaled, started crying as I felt the Holy Spirit fill me, I then said, "Oh, Thank you, Father, I'm home!" I've never felt "at home" anywhere in my life. I'd not called anywhere "home" since I was thrown out of my parents' house at age seventeen.

I cried thru the entire service. It was as if it was just for me. I felt every question I had over the past two and a half months (since the beating March 28, 2016), were being answered. Most of all, I am His, and He loves me! I left there with *hope* for the first time in a year and a half! I felt full of the Holy Spirit again, no longer was I empty, or "felt" lost and alone! The next week, the woman on the Worship Team sang "Worth" (If you have never heard the song, "Worth" by Jason Crabb, you have to go on YouTube.com and listen to this amazing song. To me, this was my song.) I'd never heard this song, but I knew the Holy Spirit was speaking to me. This had become my song.

> I came here to hide but instead was found.
> Father, thank you, for never leaving or giving up on me.

From the songs that were sung. to the pastor's message, I felt as if it was all being spoken right to my soul. I cried the entire service. Every week when I returned, more amazing messages and miracles were happening, for me. This was such a different church; the pastor didn't always have to preach. He said if the Spirit was calling for something else, we go with it; sometimes, it was a song being sung the entire time, someone else with a message at that moment, honoring the police, fire and EMT Departments. This church is "not" about the pastor; it is about God.

The third week there, the worship team played and one woman sang "Worth" by Jason Crabb. I'd never heard this song before, but I knew God was telling me this was what he'd done for me. She sang this song over and over for an hour and a half. So many of us went to the altar and prayed, and we had others pray with and over us. For me, an amazing woman named Angie prayed over and with me. The hate that I had for Scot was just too much for me to carry anymore. I'm not made to hate but to love. It was killing me, and I had to forgive him. Angie prayed with me, and I felt the hatred being removed from my soul.

Amazing people started coming into my life, and good things started happening. I had tried to leave to go to Florida or back to Kentucky, but God had other plans. He'd had them all along and had only been waiting for me. He'd placed on my heart, "Daughter, you are home for now." I know my next stop is with Him, my eternal home. I was then graced with a job of being useful to someone else. The job came from my Angel, Angie, at church. I was told I'd been an answer to their prayers! They were an answer to my prayers! I have no desire to move anywhere now. I no longer have to run. If God needs me or calls on me, I still continue to do His bidding, to do whatever He lays upon my heart.

I went back to Kentucky one weekend to see Michael graduate high school. Jim told me he'd take good care of Sam for me feeding him. At this time, Jim's girlfriend was also living there. Upon my return, Sam was missing. Jim and his girlfriend told me he'd run away. I knew they were lying. Sam had never run away, he was de-clawed, did not ever eat table food and would never be able to take care of himself. I called every SPCA and animal shelter around. I called Home Again and put up signs everywhere walking for miles looking for him every day. After a few weeks, still no Sam. I felt like part of me was gone. Some of Jim's friends and his girlfriend had told me that Jim took him and dumped him off somewhere. His friends said he goes around bragging about it. I was devastated.

I worked for Jodi for three and a half months and became friends with her and the entire family. Soon after meeting the family, they and another person I'd met got together and raised enough money for me to get an apartment in Ottawa and then on a Sunday, all at once, they came and moved me. The apartment wasn't ready, but they kept the trailers and SUV's loaded until I could move in after a couple of days. Never in my life had I met people as gracious and loving as were those now in my life. Jodi was a quadriplegic and a social worker who worked at a hospital. My job was to drive her to/from work every day and be her arms and legs while also helping her with her needs. Every time we drove through Lima, I looked for Sam but never found him.

I received a phone call at 1:35 p.m. on September 22, 2016. Someone asked if I had a missing cat. Not even two miles from where

I'd been staying they had found Sam in the Miramar warehouse hiding. They, Jim and his girlfriend, had tried to cut his chip out of him before they dumped him.

The founders at Miramar had to cut his collar from him. His name tag had my name, phone number, and his name on it, but it was embedded into his skin under his arm. He is nothing but skin and bones. I went to pick him up, and when he saw and heard me he started meowing, trying to get out a tiny hole in a box and being so excited he peed everywhere! I picked him up; Sam wrapped his little paws around my neck, rubbing my face with his, purring and meowing! The employees were saying, aw, look he knows his Mommy has him, he feels safe! Oh, I feel horrible he's in such bad condition. For now, he's eaten, drank, I've cut so much junk off of him and was going to bathe him, but he's passed out and seems to feel safe and secure for now.

Pictures of Sam before, after and now. When the people I was living with stole him and tried to cut out his chip thinking he could be tracked. The psychiatrist made Sam my Service Cat and I have a certified letter stating this.

When I was praying, I said, "Lord, you told us to cry out to you when we need you, I need you, I need a miracle about now (I have another broken down car, but I trust and believe—you've got this!" I sure didn't expect this!

Then I get another phone call telling me what vet to take him to in the morning, and the bill will be taken care of! And my little angel friends had my car temporarily fixed . . . again! My God is much bigger than anything I come across or any situation! Praise Jesus!

When I took Sam to the vet, the next morning, Deb from Deb's Dogs, met me there. The vet didn't think Sam would live. He was dehydrated, and she thought his kidneys would be affected. Sound familiar! He weighed four pounds, which is sixteen pounds lighter than the last time I saw him. He had two gaping holes in him. I was told it looked like someone tried to dig out his chip. I confirmed that because Jim's friend told me later that Jim and his girlfriend thought the chip was a tracking device and tried to dig it out but couldn't find it. The other wound was from where his tag was that had his name, my name and phone number on it. It had been embedded into his skin. Sam stayed at the Vet Clinic for a week on an IV for medicine and fluids. They'd taken only one full body x-ray and thought everything was good. However, after a few months, Sam's back right ankle was still hurting him as he kept chewing it and not walking on it. Taking him back to the vet, they took another x-ray and found it was broken. As you see in one of the pictures above, it's healed, but he can't bend it correctly to sit on it, and he limps. It doesn't matter to me; Sam is perfect just the way he is.

During my time working with Jodi, she was sick off and on. She stayed in the hospital as a patient one time, and I stayed with her. After physical therapy was done with my thumb, it still didn't move. The doctor decided it was "trigger thumb," so he did surgery. It wasn't trigger thumb either! He sent me for nerve conduction testing. The results: right anterior interosseous neurolysis, here is the medical definition of this:

The Anterior Interosseous Neurolysis (AIN) is a motor nerve innervating the deep muscles of the forearm. Anterior Interosseous Neurolysis (AIN) is a motor branch from the Median nerve and runs deep in the forearm along with the anterior interosseous artery. It innervates three muscles in the forearm. Anterior Interosseous Neurolysis (AIN) syndrome is a rare condition that comprises less than 1 percent of all upper extremity nerve palsies, arising due to compression in the upper limb.

Once again, I had to undergo surgery, and it was on Halloween day. My doctor said he'd never encountered this in his entire career and he was "the best-known hand doctor" in this area. When I came out of surgery, the doctor told me, "He must have really hurt you bad to have damaged the nerve which he did. It's very rare this nerve is ever damaged because it is so protected. It has taken me a year to gain three-fourths usage of my thumb, and that is probably all the range I'll have. Jodi's Mom, Diane (my best friend now) took Jodi to work for me while Diane's husband, Bill, took me to surgery! Bill and Diane have undoubtedly, been nothing less than a gift from God. I wasn't supposed to go right back to work but, being me, I did.

As you see, for this type of surgery, the doctor needed to cut my arm in two places for correctly fixing the problem. I still have these beautiful scars!

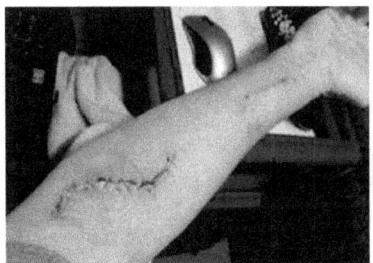 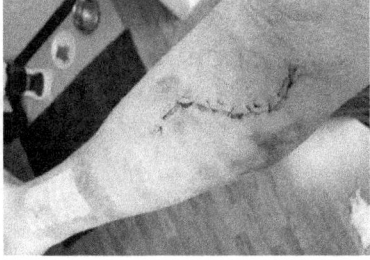

What my right arm looked like after the two surgeries.
It took a full year to begin gaining use of
my right thumb again.

I went back to work the next day, and I only took a pain pill in the morning when I got Jodi to work. Yes, I was in a little bit of pain! Jodi had some migraines that week asking for a couple of my pain pills, she said she didn't want to ask her own doctor again. Though it was wrong, and I felt bad for her, I gave her a couple. As the week went on, there were quite a few of my pain pills taken from my purse, as well as, some money. I started hiding my purse in our file cabinet, but it happened two more times. Jodi told one of the nurses who went to the head nurse, and she filed a complaint with security. Jodi and I were called back to her boss's office, told I had to come in tomorrow for a drug test, and they would run the background check that day since it had never been done. I was Jodi's employee, not theirs.

The next morning, I picked up Jodi and went to do as requested. They told me there was something bad on my federal background check, so they'd have to wait for it to see what it was. I tried to explain about the time Scot threw me out and locked the doors in the winter. I had no shoes, socks, or coat on. He called the police and because I was sitting by the road, was scared of him, they said they knew he was smoking marijuana and drinking because they saw it all in the house, but since I had nowhere to go and stay, they'd take me in to be safe. What a joke, they charged me with alcohol intoxication, but it was him drinking, not me.

The Human Resources people wouldn't listen, they didn't care. Then I was given a urine drug test; it was negative, and my urine was clear because I drink tons of water a day. The woman asked me to sit and wait. She came back with another person and said to me, "Have you been drinking this morning?" I almost fell off the chair. I replied, "No, I have to drive Jodi, and I'd never risk her life doing that."

She told me, "I smell alcohol and your urine was clear, did you drink all night?"

MY PATH OF FAITH

I'd had all I could take. I stood up and said, "No, I've not been drinking, and why is it that because I was stolen from, I'm being accused of something I've not done," and walked out of the room.

Jodi was sitting waiting for me and said, "We need to talk when we get home."

I looked at her and started to cry. I said, "Are you kidding me; you're going to fire me? I gave you some pain pills, I was the one that someone stole from, and I would never drink and drive and have not been drinking."

She said, "We'll talk when we get to my house."

I told her, "There's no need, I see what kind of friend you really are, you'd never stand up for anyone and tell the truth."

We drove to her place in silence, and when I got there, I set her up and left. I've since found out that I have a serious medical condition that makes your urine clear!

I was heartbroken. Once again, I trusted a human and became friends with them, and they let me down. I should've known better; people always fail me. No person has ever believed in me, stood up or fought for me. It has always been easier for them to abandon me. I also thought her entire family would do the same. To my surprise, Diane and Bill remained my friends! They didn't abandon me! I've told Diane more about myself then I'd ever told another human being, and she still loves me as I am! I continued helping her in her craft store, and she'd pay me so I could pay my bills. However, more than that, she's paid me so much more with her kindness and love.

What I didn't know was the apartment I was living in was consumed with mold. This too would have explained a lot if anyone would have cared to know! I was getting sicker and sicker. Every time I get sick, from mold (my biggest allergy as I said earlier), it's different, but it affects my personality, my memory, yes, I can even appear to be drunk because of the effects of it. I talked to my property owner, and he graciously allowed me out of my lease. Bill and Diane allowed me to move in with them until my new apartment would be ready at the end of November in about a month. Diane, Bill and some church friends moved all of my belongings to their garage and then cleaned the apartment.

Bill does *not* like cats, and he worked at GM, so he only has GM cars. I had a Honda and a cheap one that kept breaking down! I had a dream one night that Bill was going around saying, "Yes, hell hasn't frozen over there's a cat in my house and a Honda in my driveway!"

We all still joke about that. One of the apartments, which were going to be rented, the person backed out, so I, was allowed to move in early. To me, it was beautiful; hardwood floors, bookshelves and so big. The last one, the living room and kitchen were the same room, the bedroom and laundry room were the same room and the bathroom, and well, it was the size of a small RV bathroom! But, it was mine! This one had two bedrooms, a laundry/storage room, was beautiful, and more inexpensive than the first one! Once I was at Diane and Bill's, my health started improving. Thank you, Father, for giving me so many blessings!

I was helping Diane in her craft store, but also frantically searching for a job of my own. At the end of November, I was blessed with a security job at Menards through a security company. The job entailed that we sit at a booth outside but also greet customers outside at the gate checking them in and out with their orders. It was winter and freezing, but I didn't mind that. I love the people I'm working with and the people at Menards. Again, I love meeting new people and helping them and the shift that I'm working was perfect. I cleaned out and organized the guard booth, fixing it up nice for all of us. I'm very organized and like things in order!

MY PATH OF FAITH

Where Is God in My Path of Faith?

On this one, I don't even know where to begin. He brought me four hours away from where I'd lived since 1990 to find "my home." He gave me places to live, even if only for a short while; while the Holy Spirit filled me again and gave me the hope I'd lost so I could again find my way. He answered my prayers over and over; bringing Sam back to me was just one. Even though one person abandoned me, he showed me; it doesn't mean everyone will. But, more than anything, He had so much more planned for me that if I'd have stayed in the job with Jodi, His plans could not have happened!

Scripture

> Today I have given you the choice between life and death, between blessings and curses. Now I call on heaven and earth to witness the choice you make. Oh, that you would choose life, so that you and your descendants might live. (Deuteronomy 30:19, NLT)

Praise

Heavenly Father, I may not have had the life you planned for me, but thank you for the blessings you have given me. I am grateful I know you and will always follow you, regardless of myself. I do choose life and embrace it to the fullest!

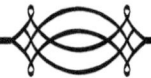

Chapter 23

God Blesses Me Abundantly beyond My Dreams

In November, I have no idea why, but I joined Our Time dating site. I didn't tell anyone and really didn't respond to anyone because I was really too scared to. Then I met a man, we started talking, and he started calling me.

His name was Steve; he also worked at GM as Bill previously did. I joked and told Diane and Bill, "If I were ever going to be with another man, I want him to be like Bill, a good down to earth, Christian, and honest man." Steve and I talked for a month on the phone before we met. He'd worked at GM for thirty-nine years, and most of the time, he worked seven days a week, twelve–fourteen hours a day on third shift. He wanted to go out, but I said I would cook dinner for us. I felt I'd have more control that way! He came over, and we ate and talked. I felt like I'd known him all my life and to be honest; this scared me! A couple of hours into our date, we were sitting on the couch talking, and I said to him, "I feel comfortable enough with you; I have something to tell you." He asked what it was.

I said, "Reach between the cushions on my right." He did as I asked and started laughing. I'd stashed my handgun there loaded for my protection. Steve told me he was happy to see that I could look out for myself!

We couldn't get enough of each other, and we talked several times a day and during the night. By January, he'd asked me to marry him. We'd discussed everything, and I'd prayed so much to see if this was God's will and not mine. I'd made a promise to God, and I intended to keep it. If this weren't God's will, I wouldn't do it no matter what. I had so many signs telling me it was God's will that I could no longer deny it. I'd introduced him to Diane and Bill, and they actually knew each other! The amazing part that we learned, they are like brothers. They are so much alike!

I'd had one request of Steve, and it was that we keep ourselves pure until we were married. I had done my other relationships wrong, and I wanted this to be right since it was from God. He had no problem agreeing! I felt as if I found my long lost best friend/soul mate. There is nothing either of us can do to make the other not love each other. How amazing is this! God does do miracles! I can't believe God moved me all the way here to find Steve!

I was having trouble again with asthma/allergies. The guard booth at work had mold, and my employers said they believe it was just dirt from the rain. I was getting so bad that I couldn't breathe. I was delirious and having some heart problems. I was told by my doctor to quit, which I did. Steve and I were trying to decide when to get married. He paid my February rent, and I asked if I could move in March. We'd decided we would marry in March. We were receiving so much feedback from church (I was now at a "different church") and others having a hard time arranging a date that I had to move in with Steve, and we wanted still to remain pure.

He had some vacation time; Diane and Bill were already in Venice, Florida, for the month of February, and I had a brilliant idea! We called Diane and Bill and arranged to visit them, and then be married on February 6, 2017, at the courthouse with them as our witnesses. We told no one what we were doing! We had a wonderful time, it was a beautiful week of bliss, and it has only continued. I would never have picked anyone as wonderful as God provided. I am truly blessed now with my new friends and husband.

My Wedding with Steve and our witnesses, Bill and Diane Rieman.

Steve and I laugh like two high school kids and have so much fun. One day, we were in a store grocery shopping, laughing, teasing each other and having our usual fun, and a customer came up to us and asked if we were just friends or dating because we looked like we were having so much fun. We told her we were married

Steve and I being married! I am truly blessed.

and just love being with each other and having fun. She commented, "I remember when my husband and I use to be like that. Maybe we need it back." She walked away while Steve and I hugged and kissed each other. Thank you again, Heavenly Father, for shining through us and allowing others to see you through us.

My life is still not perfect by any means; after all, we are human. My daughter and older son still do not talk to me ,but my youngest, Michael, we talk almost every day. He is truly a reflection of Christ. No, I don't think he's perfect, he's not a mama's boy, he just makes his life all about God and has since he was able to talk and, honestly, I'd say before he was born.

I still pray for Tina and Scotty, someday hoping to hold them again in my arms and meet their loved ones and families if they have one. I know I've hurt and exposed them to a life full of things they shouldn't have been exposed to but more than anything, I'd love to talk to them about it, as we used to. However, that is all up to the Heavenly Father now.

When I meet parents, and they tell me their story, whether female or male, and they say the kids have no idea of what really happened, and I don't want them ever to think of their other parent like that. I tell them, if your daughter and/or sons are old enough to understand the truth, trust me, they already know, but they probably don't really know the truth just what their own mind forms. You need to sit down and talk to them, honestly. Don't do it with vengeance and hate in your heart, but instead, ask them to pray with you first, about what you need to talk to them about, and then speak with love in your heart. Let them ask questions, don't place blame or ask for pity, just tell it as this is what happened, and I want to tell you so you can learn how *not* to let it happen in your life.

We are to teach our children right from wrong. I thought that by not telling them everything, they didn't see it or really know what was going on. They didn't know all of what was going on, but they knew it what they did see wasn't right either and that I, nor they, should be there either nor should be treated as we were being treated. That's a lot for children to comprehend. I should know, I went through it too! Then, as a lot of us do, we block it out of our minds and then that parent becomes the bad guy. I should have seen this, but I was so wrapped up in protecting myself and, I thought, them, that I was really hurting all of us. I tried to be open and honest with all of them, but I was so messed up myself from my childhood and felt so unloved how could I have really been a good mother? So, I give God all the credit for how my children turned out, not me. The three of them hate me to this day. My daughter doesn't even speak to me; she found another woman to be her mom.

My son seeks a mother figure through the women he falls in love with and lets them run his life instead of being the man that he really is and my other son, well, hopefully, God is protecting him from being abused by his father now. My other son, well, I know, God is protecting him, and he is walking a true path of faith, and I know he tries to love me. Don't get me wrong, I will love my children always. In my eyes, they are the world to me no matter if they hate me or don't understand. I am still so proud of the adults that they have become and that is only because they are each beautiful individuals in their own way. It doesn't matter what they do in life for a living, it is who they are to me. I just pray that they are a good people, treat others with respect and kindness. More than anything, I just want them to be happy, truly happy in life, and find all of the love that God has to offer.

My heart is always God first; take care of myself, my husband, and my kids. My only dream for my life was to have kids, once they grew up, be friends with them and a part of their lives.

I prayed this day asking for their love, if not for me then for each other. If I could hold each one of them in my arms just one more time to tell them I love them and how much God loves them, and if Tina, too, could find her way back to God, I'd be willing to give my life for them so that they may all live in everlasting peace and love with Christ. I know His love; I felt it again this day. I want that for all three of my children, as well as Amanda, Scotty's girlfriend, and Jake, Tina's boyfriend. Oh, how I'd love to meet Jake, Tina's boyfriend, just to see the man my little girl fell in love with!

Where Is God in My Path of Faith?

God showed me the way and gave me the signs. I was willing not to go my way if it was not of him. He's shown me so much love and blessings over the past year. At times, I become so overwhelmed because I never knew life could be this happy. The best of all, the Heavenly Father brought me the most amazing man to love me and show me how a man really loves a woman as his wife, and he is teaching me how to truly love a man as my husband.

Scripture

> In the same way, there is joy in the presence of God's angels when even one sinner repents. (Luke 15:10, NLT)
>
> God's way is perfect. All the Lord's promises prove true. He is a shield for all who look to him for protection. (Psalm 18:30, NLT)

Praise

Father, I thank you for never giving up on me or leaving me. Instead, you brought me home. You answered my prayers, and you heard my cries; now I am giving you my life for all of eternity to serve you. I pray this in Jesus' Name. One day, bringing Jodi home, she'd asked what I had hope in. My response to her, "I have no hope in anything. I just serve God and do whatever is needed of me. I know better than to hope."

Jodi said, "Barbie. You have to hope in something!"

I replied' "No, I don't. I cannot anymore."

Shortly after this conversation is when Sam was found, I met my husband, and my life has been forever changed. Lord, thank you for giving me back "hope!"

Chapter 24

Making My Peace with the Past

Recently, God had placed it on my heart to find my mother and go to her and make peace for my family. That my family will not heal if I don't deal with her before it's too late (she's ninety). In two days, I found her and went. She's in a nursing home.

Steve told me not to be disappointed! I told him I couldn't be, I'm not doing this expecting anything! I'm doing it because I'm obeying what I've been told to do! I wanted her to know that I forgive her and that I know she did the best she could with what she had. That I am sorry I disappointed her as her child, but God loves me, and I love her as Jesus loves her. God speaks, and I jump. This has always been my life purpose. I think some people think I'm crazy, or just don't quite understand when I say this! I don't try and explain it, and I never have.

It went just as I expected. She said she suffered a horrible life, I was a horrible child and that I took Dad's side, but she remembers the day God got her off alcohol. She's a different person now and doesn't want to think about her past because she failed with her family, but has a wonderful God-given family that loves her there at the nursing home! It's the only family, which matters to her! She said I went to Dad because of his power and money, and I took his money!

I gently reminded her of the money he gave her and my siblings. She said I don't want to talk about this! The patient techs said they look for her to die someday this year.

All I could think of while talking to her was this could be my children and me sitting here talking. She said things happened that she'd never tell me about why she felt the way she did. I told her I completely understand why. My daughter doesn't talk to me because of decisions I made, and not talking to them. So, maybe if you'd have talked to us, we'd have understood. Fear makes us do things we don't want to do. She said, "She doesn't talk to you?"

I said no. Mom just smiled.

I said that's why I'm here to make peace, to break this cycle you've created of disowning family members. I'll listen to what I've done wrong, explain my decisions, and try to make amends for the future with my children—they are my God-given Family. I told my youngest, Michael, all of this. I said, "Sorry if this is too much, but I just want you to know I am trying to grow. I live a Christ-filled life and God is always first."

There's one other thing Mom said to me. She said she knows what it's like now for the first time to be loved unconditionally because of the people at the nursing home.

I replied, "Oh, I know exactly what you mean!"

She replied, "What do you mean? I loved you unconditionally."

At that point, all I thought to myself was say a prayer, "I too thought I loved my children unconditionally. But, how could I, if I didn't know myself what it was or how to even love?" I asked Christ to please forgive me for my wrong ways of thinking and show me His Way.

I went to her because I was told to. I thought it was for healing for her. and I, instead, received insight into me as a person and a mother. I tried to do and be what she wasn't, but I guess some things I just didn't see yet. I'm grateful, no matter the pain to me, for the knowledge Christ reveals to me.

Where Is God in My Path of Faith?

God tells me to go, and I obey, then he teaches me more about myself. I may never see Mom again or know when she passes, but I obeyed and made my peace.

Scripture

> For God speaks again and again, though people do not recognize it. (Job 33:14, NLT)
> So Moses told the people, "You must be careful to obey all the commands of the Lord your God, following his instructions in every detail." (Deuteronomy 5:32, NLT)

Praise

Heavenly Father, thank you for showing me the truth of myself the way to Your Light, and for giving me opportunities to bless others but more importantly to walk in Your Truth and obey You.

Chapter 25

Jesus Continues to Visit and Now I Listen

On August 24, 2017, I awoke from a dream where Steve and I were taking my daughter and Mom somewhere fun for the evening. Mom wanted Steve to do something for her, so we went to our house. Tina was sitting at the piano (which we don't have), and she said, "Mom, please don't hate me, I think I've become you."

I touched the side of her face and hair gently replying, "Oh, sweetheart, no you haven't, you are your own beautiful self. Take ownership of that and have a wonderful life. You, Tina Habig, are a beautiful, amazing person, and I love you very much just as you are."

Then I went into where Mom was sitting, telling her about what happened to Sam and I. Mom then asked me, "Are you okay now?"

I told her we are. When she looked down at me, she had so much love in her eyes. I had never seen that look in her eyes for me. She looked as if she wanted to hug me, but didn't know how. I told her, "Mom, it's all right, I forgave you long ago. Jesus showed me how to love you just as you are through His eyes."

I woke up and thought, I wonder if Mom is passing away soon, but I'll never know because my brothers and sister won't tell me. Then, my next thought was, maybe it's me that's going to pass away since I saw both of them or am I just at peace with them now!

I've been waking up every night around 2:55 a.m. for the last month, and August 25, 2017, was no exception. The only difference was as I lay in our camper bed looking out the window the devil appeared. He was burning red, and red flames were shooting off of him. I started praying, "I rebuke the devil and all evil in the name of Jesus Christ." I prayed this over and over until he faded away, and the face of Jesus appeared. I felt Him tell me, "You must hurry and finish your book, your time is almost up."

I felt His love again like I always have but knew, without a doubt this was my last mission and calling; that this book was to be written for His Glory, not mine and for a greater purpose.

Thank you, Heavenly Father, for all of the love You've given me. I've been told that my dream means spiritual healing for me with my daughter and Mom. Shortly after these occurrences, I was led to go to God as my judge and repented all of my sins and prayed to break all of my agreements and bonds of those from my ancestors to my children who have brought curses down on me in the past, present, and future, including myself.

I broke all agreements with death and evil. I've let each of those people go and take their own baggage. Most of all, I've gone before God as my Judge, with Jesus as my mediator and asked for the freedom to forgive myself for all of my mistakes, shame, and pride, which led me down all the wrong paths in my life. Whether these were from ancestor curses, my mom, or whomever that had stolen so much of my life, I forgive them all and myself and give them back what is theirs.

In May of 2018 I went to visit my mom for what would be my final visit. Upon my arrival she immediately called her pastor to come, I'm assuming, to protect her from me. While talking, she told me again, in her words and with disgust and a look of hatred for me on her face, she said; "you and your father ruined my life. Bonnie said everyone in Loveland knew about it." I asked her, how and what did everyone know about? But then Pastor walked in and everything changed, even her look of hate for me on her face. I just felt more compassion for this woman who God had given me to be my mother.

I said to her; "Mom my reason for this visit was to thank you for being my mother. God knew what He was doing when he appointed you my mother because if it weren't for him and you I would not be the person I am today. So, thank you for being my mother and I am sorry for whatever hurt it is that I caused you."

After leaving her that day and on my sixteen hour drive, I prayed that God would please help her soul to find peace and to know his love as I do. When I looked into this women's eyes, whom I once called mom, I could see how tormented her soul was and it broke my heart hurting for her.

In August of 2018, the woman, Anne Schuchart, who took on the role of being my mother in this life even though as I've learned after her funeral, she did not give birth to me. My one brother and sister (mom's children) Steve and Debi, and her family; and my half-brother, Jimmy (who'd already told me where to go in a text message) would not even look at, let alone come near my husband and me. Mom's Pastor said it would never change, they will always be that way towards me. Pastor said after all the years of being mom's caregiver, he was dismissed by my brother being told, he now has control over the money. I told Pastor, I came to her funeral only because of God's laws. He says we are to honor our parents. I was there to honor and pay my respects. I didn't want her money or worldly possessions.

I asked Pastor if my mom had ever told him anything about Dad having an affair and having me. He said, "you really don't look like any of them do you." Then his answer to my question was this, "let's just say, Annie went to her grave with some deep, dark secrets." At that moment, I felt the all so familiar warm, white light overcome me, and it was as if God was reaching down and lifting the entire world off of me. I had this overwhelming powerful understanding that, "oh that explains everything!" My next thought was what an amazing woman to take me in and raise me, oh how I wished she'd not had so much hate in her heart for me. Just then pastor's wife walked up and said, you don't look a thing like them or your mom, you must take after your Dad and his side of the family. I have since found out through a DNA test that Anne was never my biological mother. Apparently, Dad had an affair with his ex-wife, and she got pregnant while Anne and Dad were married. Anne was pregnant at the time I was to be born also but as I'm told she had a miscarriage, went into the hospital and when she came home she brought me with her. My Mom, Deloris Brauckman, was a famous singer in Vegas and she also left my sister, Carin to be cared for by our Grandmother. I was able to meet Carin one time and we talked for four hours and sadly three days later she passed away. I did have the pleasure of meeting my mother at Carin's funeral but that was 21 years ago, and I knew of none of this then.

Do I feel upset about being given away? No way! I feel so free! I'm so grateful that God has revealed all of the truth to me and that I am now finally able to be all that he wants me to be! I knew it was never me who ruined Anne's life, but I never understood why I was so unlovable to her! God loves me and for me, that is enough to make me complete! However, now I do know why God placed it on my heart to thank her for being my mother and no matter what I am grateful Anne was my mother because God gave me her for a reason! Thank you, Father, for the mom you gave me!

Where Is God in My Path of Faith?

Christ never fails or falters to show up when I need him most. Can you see where he showed up and gave me exact directions? He even tells me who and when to talk with.

MY PATH OF FAITH

Scripture

> For everything there is a season, a time for every activity under heaven. (Ecclesiastes 3:1, NLT)

Praise

I might not have had the life you planned out for me, but You were with me through every moment of it, never failing me.

BARBIE SCHUCHART-CARLISLE

Christ in Me

Be as simple as you can be;
You will be astonished to see
How uncomplicated and happy your life can be.

Giving unconditional love to all,
Following the love of God, and
Loving through Jesus' eyes,
Seeing His presence in everyone,
Just where they are.

That is the way to live.
Touch me, O God, to shine
With Your confidence, love, and happiness
In the garden of my life
So that others may see Your light in me
And;
Want to follow along Your path because of You in me.

Barbie Carlisle
August 23, 2017

Chapter 26

Is This the End?

In Christ, we are to become God's "living sacrifice." *"And so, dear brothers and sisters, I plead with you to give your bodies to God because of all he has done for you. Let them be a living and holy sacrifice— the kind He will find acceptable. This is truly the way to worship him"* (*Romans 12:1*). I've said many times to my Savior and Lord and continue to on a daily basis. That one day in the hospital, I totally surrendered my all to Him. I used to "think I trusted Him," but when it was the darkest, a lot of times, I gave up, thinking I was alone. Forgetting I'm never alone.

Today, I'm facing some difficult medical diagnosis that I've probably had for many years. For the first time in my life, my first reaction is "God, I'm not giving up this time! I trust You. Whatever You want me to do, I am willing." I know, without a doubt in my heart and soul, He *will* "transform" me by renewing my mind, body, and spirit for whatever He needs me to focus on for the things that please Him. Wow! What a revelation and change for me! Amen! Thank you, Jesus!

It's helpful to know that God will never call on us to do something for which He has not already equipped us. As Paul reminds us, *"In his grace, God has given us different gifts for doing certain things well"* (*Romans 12:6, NLT*). I know God has given me more grace than anyone deserves! There's no doubt He will equip you and me to do anything that He calls on us to do! Do not ever doubt this!

Heavenly Father, no one deserves our sacrifice and dedication more than You. Help us to realize the joy that comes from abandoning ourselves to You. I do not doubt that this *is not* the life, which you had chosen for me that I created most of what I had to live through. Once I dedicated myself to You and was a willing vessel (and even unknowingly willing), I allowed you to use my life for others to see and learn of You, as well as for me to see You in my life.

Once you've completely abandoned yourself to Him, all that is left for you to give of yourself is "love through Jesus' eyes." When you're able to do this, you'll know you've completely abandoned yourself to your Heavenly Father.

There is no risk in abandoning ourselves to God. Once you've done this, you're in for the most amazing journey of your entire life. The blessings—you may have to search for thru the mess along your road—but in the end, you will look back and see just who carried you and was *always with you* along this beautiful journey of "My Path of Faith" and yours!

Thank you, Heavenly Father, for always being with me, whether holding my hand, at my side, or allowing me to run far ahead of you until I had to stop and wait on my knees, crying for you because I remembered that it is only You that I truly need; in every moment, but especially when I was weak. It was then that you picked me up and carried me, always showing me Your grace and love. I love you, my sweet Jesus!

Chapter 27

Who Am I Now?

My simplistic answer to this question is this:

It is not who am I, but who have I grown to become.

My truest, purest, nonnegotiable identity is my Beloved Lord. And in spite of my checkered past, my fabulous flops, my painful history, my deepest flaws, my boneheaded screw-ups, and, yes, even beyond my own beliefs about myself—I am God's beloved child. This is my foundational identity and the foundational identity of every human being.

This is important because identity is everything that drives the relationship not only with me but also with God, others and within ourselves. If your identity is broken, your life is broken. If you define it incorrectly, you will carry that wrong definition into your story. If all you see are your limitations, you will miss all of the stunning, miraculous possibilities, which God is creating right in front of, and within each one of you. All of my prayers and blessings are for each one of you, and I pray that you, too, may find "your path of faith" as you go on your journey through life.

I leave you now with one last poem that I wrote four years ago and then accidentally came across it, not remembering that I wrote it, as I was finishing this book! I made a few changes to it because all I could think was "wow, how appropriate for the end of 'My Path of Faith!'" My Father knew right where I was going to be and what I was going to be doing four years after I wrote this poem!

Always remember, The Lord Himself said, "For I know the plans I have for you," says the Lord. "They are plans for good and not for disaster, to give you a future and a hope" (Jeremiah 29:11 NLT).

Seek Him, talk, sing, pray, and praise Him. If you have to, yell at Him or cry out to Him; He will be there for you, just ask Him! He loves you!

Epilogue

It's Only the Beginning

All I Left Undone Is Now Done

>I thought I was doing so well
>Doing Your work,
>Living Your word
>Walking Your path
>There was so much to do
>When those close passed,
>My best friend came to you too -
>I lost what I thought was my calling.
>So, I just stopped living.
>
>I was broken and lost,
>Living in fear;
>Left with no hope;
>Feeling, completely alone
>Then evil found me, once again
>I took its outreached flames
>And walked away
>With so much left undone to do.
>
>I tried to end my life,
>To be with You.
>But, You called out my name,
>And You brought me back.
>You said to me. . .

"I'm not finished with you yet.
Your work here is not yet complete."
You brought me back,
From the depths of hell.

You gave me hope,
Love, strength, and courage.
You let me know,
There's so much left
For me to do;
Your path, I needed to walk.
Now I've taken,
Your outreached hand -
And together,
We've accomplished
All I Left Undone.

It's not the end of my life. It's only the Beginning!

Barbie Schuchart-Carlisle

Note:
Written: *May 5, 2013*
Revised when I found this poem again during completing of his book on: *May 5, 2017*

> *"But my life is worth nothing to me unless I use it for finishing the work assigned me by the Lord Jesus— the work of telling others the Good News about the wonderful grace of God. (Acts 20:24, NLT).*

God thought I was worth saving and told me I'm not done yet, I have work to do, his love to share! This is only the beginning!

www.ingramcontent.com/pod-product-compliance
Lightning Source LLC
Chambersburg PA
CBHW071918290426
44110CB00013B/1397